To Cher

Taking Her to the Door

The day cancer came knocking

***

John Magee

JMMagee

*I hope you enjoy
the book and
you take something
Positive from the Story*

First edition February 2020 | Published by John Magee
ISBN 978-1-9997011-2-3

Cover design and layout: Arthur Luke - www.arthurluke.co.uk
Cover photography: Ricardo Moura
Edited by: Gillian McGuiness
Proof reader: Scott Lowe

This book is dedicated to the most amazing lady in my life, who taught me the true value of Kindness. See you at the door, Mum.

We did it, Mum, we did it together. RIP
Patricia Ann Magee
9/9/1943 - 24/10/2018

I was first introduced to John when I received a heartfelt message after he had just finished watching our documentary *Be Here Now - The Andy Whitfield Story*. He later sent through, along with a copy of his book *Kindness Matters*, a handwritten letter. In the letter, along with his heartfelt message, was a humorous description of how he had forgotten the letter on his way to mail his book, but how he had chosen instead, despite the extra time it would take, to go all the way back home so as to include it. His reasoning for doing so was what grabbed me at first instance about John. His genuine kindness, compassion and desire to deeply and selflessly impact others, is not only what he does, but quite simply who he is. *Taking Her to the Door*, from conception to completion is yet another layer of the legacy of a man who wishes nothing other than to quite simply enable, support and kindly empower others while navigating the often isolating challenges of life, loss, grief and letting go. As authentic as it is genuine and as simple as it is informative, *Taking Her to the Door* shines a very poignant light on the unpredictable emotional journey of loss, grief and healing. Along with the all-important message that, while you may very much feel it, you are not alone.

Vashti Whitfield.
Be Here Now - The Andy Whitfield Story - Netflix

There are moments in life beyond our control. Even those with deep-seated faith can go into a tailspin when those dearest to them are torn away, leaving hearts bewildered and minds painfully stunned. John Magee takes us by the hand on his journey through the uninvited "new normal" with gratitude and grace that acts as a soothing balm for our wounded hearts and as a light that finally starts to shine down that long dark tunnel. *Taking Her to the Door* is an amazing message of how "hope is a rebellion", an uprising against even the worst of circumstances.

Artemis Skye McNeil, author of Her (Oscar) Wilde Heart and Keys of Love

When I first met John over 10 years ago I somehow felt like we were already friends. And today we most certainly are. He is an incredible individual with a passion for life and empowering others. His latest book *Taking Her to the Door* is a mixture of sadness and hope. How John cared for his mother in her final moments is a shining example of what unconditional love really means.

Richard McCann, author of Just a Boy

John Magee is like a fast flowing river of cosmic energy and love, overflowing with the milk of human kindness! Ready to gather up anyone that stands still in his path John has the power to carry you through your own, often turbulent journey of life with a sense of self-belief, fun and foaming positivity. You know when you are in the midst of his flow!

In John's personal and deeply touching book *Taking Her to the Door*, you really feel John's own life river flowing deeply with and from his mother's love. But on its twisting, turning journey through rapids, rocks and ravines, this river starts to silt up with fear, pain, anger, loss and grief, slowing to a stop and stagnation. Then, pouring its path into a new direction, this river emerges back into the light in full flow with the foaming, white water wisdom of a reborn man, and filled with the desire to pour the milk of human kindness into every corner of life's landscape. Let yourself be carried by his river.

Scott Lowe, www.myogabody.co.uk

I first met John over five years ago when he introduced his 'Kindness Matters' to our school. Throughout this time he has shown kindness and compassion to those he has worked with and helped. In John's book, *Taking Her to the Door,* he reveals a different side, one in which he struggles to deal with the devastating impact of the death of a parent. Having suffered the loss of a parent myself, it had great resonance and helped me reflect on my own process of grieving. John gives a thoughtful and emotional account of how cancer affected his life. His personal experiences, reflection and positive mind-set give the reader an insight into how a devastating loss can bring growth and hope for the future.

Gillian McGuinness

Taking Her to the Door is a warm hug of hope when you are at your darkest times. John Magee demonstrates how light does find a way and how there are great lessons in unexpected and unimaginable circumstances. This book is strength, grace and kindness to keep you moving forward when you feel like it's hard to take one step.

Amberly Lago, author of *True Grit and Grace*

'There is nothing more certain and unchanging than uncertainty and change.'
John F. Kennedy

***

We all have goals in life – hopes, aspirations and dreams we work towards. Often we share these things with the people whom we love the most as we journey through life.

The thing is though, when cancer comes to knock at your door, all these hopes and dreams evaporate into the ether, and you find yourself caught up in a whirlwind of thoughts and emotions. It's like a bad dream from which you cannot awake.

This is my story of when cancer knocked at our door.

My Mum, also known as Nana Pat, was diagnosed with terminal throat cancer on the 26th July 2018 and with that diagnosis came the information that her life expectancy was very short.

I loved Mum more than can be put into words. She was the kindest and most generous person I have ever known. She would do anything for anyone, living her life with her heart on her sleeve. But cancer didn't care about any of that. It didn't care that she had children. It didn't care for her grandchildren. It didn't care for anyone or anything.

When you are given the news of cancer, reality kicks in.

All your hopes and dreams, those things you have built your life around, no longer seem important. What matters is the remaining time you and your loved ones have together. Your only thoughts are of how you will spend the short, precious time together.

My Mum, like most people who have been diagnosed with terminal cancer, was in shock. She wasn't ready to die and was desperate for more time. As a Catholic, she prayed for this. She wanted more memories and more special occasions with her family.

As a unit, we were all in shock too. The grandchildren were devastated. I felt like I had been thrown out into the darkness but couldn't help believe that there had to be a faint light at the end of this very dark tunnel.

Light does find a way.

You, dear reader, will get through this painful transition. You will balance your grief. It will take time – your own time. By focusing on the positives you had and not the loss - which I know is easier said than done – and taking life one day at a time, you'll get through this.

My Mum didn't want us to be sad when her time came, and, as a parent, when my own time comes, I will not want my children to be upset. Instead, I'll want to celebrate with them all the good memories of the times we'd had together.

Whether it's your partner, parent, child, family member or friend who has terminal cancer, I hope this book gives you hope and strength as you grieve and transition in your own time.

***

I remember the day the idea came to me to write this book. It was one of those very dark days despite it being August and a sunny Monday morning. Mum was in a bad way. I was feeling hopeless. I remember standing outside of her ground floor flat when my phone rang. It was a good friend Ray asking if I wanted to go for a walk with him. I wasn't in the mood for company or to talk to anyone so I politely thanked my friend and declined the offer. I hung up the phone, took a deep breath, then heard a voice.

"Write a book, John. Help others with what your mum is going through. Cancer."

I looked down at my phone to check that I had indeed hung up properly but the screen was black. I'd definitely heard a voice say those words, though. The words had been spoken very softly, but with complete clarity.

You may be a tad cynical at this stage. I don't want to sound like I am some sort of shaman or psychic or anything. I am quite a spiritual person though and had already written a book a few years earlier, 'Kindness Matters', based on the principles my mum believed in. I'd written that book to help others, and now it seemed that someone was trying to tell me to do it again.

I knew that if I wrote a book, the money raised would go straight to the facility that cared so intensively for my Mum in her final weeks, days and moments - The East Lancashire Hospice. The Hospice could benefit from the funds from sales, plus those reading the book could feel prepared and healed, and I, myself, would also heal from the process of having written everything down. For me, the chance to create positive outcomes from this truly awful situation meant I had to try. I had to write a book.

Everything I share in this book is from true life experience, but I have researched what's out there to help support you and your loved ones through this most challenging of times. I have put my heart and soul into this book and hope it gives you hope and strength.

Although I have never met you in person, I hope that *Taking Her to the Door* gives you and those you love the hope and strength you need right now. Your loved one will always be with you, every single day, in thoughts and spirit, and, as long as you keep those fond memories of good times alive, that spirit will stay with you.

When we choose to focus on what we've gained rather than what we have lost, the process of moving forward begins and allows us to share the time we have left with the people who love us.

I finish by sharing a message I received just before my Mum took her last breath in this life. It's a beautiful quote that my friend Debbie Wright sent to me, just as I was preparing to take my Mum to the door...

"Let her wings grow, and she will decide when to fly. One thing you can be sure of is that you will always find an angel by your side."

Contents

Finding a Lump

***

That day started like all the others. As I woke that morning and prepared for my day ahead I had no idea that this would be the start of a long and gruelling journey.

Like most people I was caught up in the daily grind of the rat race, rushing from one place to another as well as work, family and life commitments. For me, working in schools as a motivational speaker, my job is perhaps more varied but in many ways just as routine.

I'm an early riser, up at 5am and then my 'miracle morning routine' - yoga, meditation, reading, journaling, affirmations and silence before my busy day starts. There's something very peaceful about getting up early in the morning, having a couple of hours to myself before getting out on the road and working in schools. I haven't got a scratch on Mum though - she is known for getting up at 2:30am for a cup of tea and watching the news!

Mum's health had deteriorated over the last few years and I

had made the decision to live closer to her home. It had been a wrench to move from the lovely neighbourhood of Feniscowles, with its green fields, cricket club and quiet community, to a more, let's say, 'colourful' area of town right in the heart of Blackburn town centre, dominated by social housing and social deprivation. Even the dogs walked around in gangs! But it was for Mum, not for me at the end of the day, and I knew I couldn't have forgiven myself if I'd not been there for Mum as her health failed.

Lately work had been taking me to Blackpool, which meant I had to be on the road early. I would pop round to Mum's, make her a brew (made with two teabags and just a splash of milk stirred to the left), do any chores around the house and wish her a good day. I'd always touch base with her during the daytime as well as call in later after work.

That morning had been like all others - until mid-morning when my Auntie Muriel (or Auntie Moo to me) phoned. We had always had that special close relationship built on silly names, banter and love.

"How are you doing George?"

"Not so bad Auntie Olive," I replied. When I call at her home and press on the intercom buzzer, I always say 'It's your favourite nephew', and she says, 'Who? George?' and I'll reply,

'Yes. Is that my favourite Auntie Olive?' Then we'd always laugh together, as it's our private family joke.

This morning though my Auntie Moo didn't sound her normal chirpy self. I sensed straight away that she was worried about something.

"Have you spoken to your Mum?" I told her that I had. "Well did she tell you about the lump in her neck?"

Mum hadn't said a word and me being me said, "I'm sure it will be something or nothing but I will speak to Mum and see what is going on."

I phoned Mum straight away and asked her about the lump in her neck.

Mum being Mum said, "It's nothing. Don't you worry yourself. Get yourself to work and I will speak with Elaine the district nurse about it." There she was protecting me even though I was a grown man.

That weekend, when I had more time to spend with Mum I said, "Let's have a look at this lump on your neck."

I could not believe it. The lump was the size of a golf ball. I had a strange sinking feeling in the pit of my stomach, which was like a sixth sense. I knew Elaine, Mum's district nurse, had to look at it as soon as possible.

My Mum loved Elaine and all the district nurse team, but

especially Elaine. Elaine had looked after my Mum for years, monitoring her type two diabetes, visiting regularly with their private joke about her looking at Mum's bottom for bed sores - Mum would have extensive periods sat in her favourite chair facing the window.

When Elaine came round to look at the lump on Mum's neck, her face was like a book. "John, I want the doctor out as soon as possible", she exclaimed.

The doctor arrived within the hour and started asking questions.

"Have you ever smoked Patricia?"

Mum had smoked sixty a day for most of her life but she had stopped ten years ago after having had a serious stroke.

As the doctor started asking more questions I knew what her thoughts were. At that moment I felt overwhelmed with emotion, a voice in my head saying "No, no, this can't be what I think it is… we don't have this in our family…what about the grandkids?..." My thoughts started to race but thankfully I did my best to bring myself back into the moment.

And then the doctor said the word which caused ice to run through my veins.

"Just to be safe, I would like to book you into the hospital to make sure it is not cancer."

And at very that moment my world changed.

It's Cancer

***

The next few days seemed to go by with a sense of unreality. On the one hand, you convince yourself that it's probably nothing but on the other, deep down, you know you're fooling yourself.

The following week I took the day off work to take Mum to her appointment at Blackburn Royal Hospital. Like many hospitals, the entrance was a structure of glass and open space, dominated by sunlight. Behind this façade there is a sobering truth - so many old people lying in beds, clinging on to life. And then there are the young children, wheelchair-bound with tubes and wires obscuring their young faces. Hospitals always seem to ground me, make me realise how grateful I need to be. There are so many people in much worse positions than me.

As we made our way through the busy hospital, the smell of illness and disinfectant in the air, we bumped into a couple of friends I'd grown up with - Tommy and Davie - brothers who worked as porters in the hospital. Their faces lit up when they saw Mum, remembering her character and personality from their childhoods.

"You must be proud of your lad, Mrs Magee, an author and all that. I always thought I would bump into him in jail!" joked Tommy. But as we laughed and joked I could see the tension in Mum's face, knowing that we were minutes away from meeting the specialist, Doctor Mahmood.

Sitting Mum down, I got her booked in with the kind looking receptionist and joined her on the waiting area seats. Sensing the tension and nervousness I started a bit of banter with Mum – to calm my nerves as much as hers. Being brought up in an Irish family getting the 'craic' going was how it worked but I could tell Mum just wanted to get the appointment over and done with. What she really wanted was the all-clear.

As we waited for her name to be called Mum's anxiety increased. Mum has suffered from agoraphobia for years and it's easy to spot her stress levels increasing. First, she becomes quiet – the calm before the storm. Then the fidgeting starts which quickly turns into cursing and then the demands to leave and return home.

Mum started getting agitated and frustrated.

Suddenly she said, "If I have to wait any bloody longer you

can take me home!"

"Shut your cakehole, Mum," I said affectionately. It was essential that she had this appointment.

'I'll do more than shut your cakehole if you carry on talking like that to me!"

Mum and I always had this kind of banter - it was our way of giving each other a bit of jip with no harm meant.

Again as we waited, the nervousness started to creep back in. I said to Mum, "Why don't we do a RAOK, a 'Random Act Of Kindness'?"

She asked me what I was thinking of doing. There was a table near the reception with books and magazines for people to read whilst they were waiting.

"Why don't I nip back to the car and put a signed copy of 'Kindness Matters' on the table? Whilst I'm down there I'll get you a brew with two tea bags in it and I will stir it to the left, just as you like it." As you know my Mum loves a strong brew with only a drop of milk.

I came back with the builder's brew and in my book, I wrote this message: "If you read any act of kindness that touches your heart within this book why not pay that kind act forward. Thank you for your kindness," and I placed it on the table. To our surprise five minutes later a young, dark-haired nurse approached us, clutching my book in her hand.

"Have you just put this book on the table over there?" she asked with a lovely smile on her face.

"Yes, why?" I replied.

"This is lovely...," she said. But before she could finish her sentence, my Mum, with such pride in her voice, said, "It's my son who wrote that book called 'Kindness Matters'. He is an author."

"Be quiet Mum!" I said.

The nurse asked if this was true and I explained that Mum and I wanted to pay forward a copy of the book for all the patients in the reception with a hope that it would inspire anyone who picked it up to do an act or two of kindness.

The nurse asked if she and all her team could read it first, as it is something they do daily to make patients feel better. Well, you should have seen my Mum's face. It was a picture. I agreed and then before we knew it, the receptionist shouted, "Mrs Magee for Doctor Mahmood."

We made our way to see Doctor Mahmood. He was a lovely man, very smartly dressed with a lovely, calm smile. With him was an assistant, a tall blonde haired woman, a nurse I assumed, who spoke softly to Mum with a patient and professional manner and a reassuring smile on her face.

Doctor Mahmood glanced at the notes, adjusted his glasses and then asked Mum if she had ever smoked. She explained that back in the day she would have sixty plus cigarettes a day, but she had stopped in 2009 due to having the stroke.

"So when did you first notice the lump in your neck?" he asked gently.

"A couple of weeks ago," she replied.

The doctor looked a little shocked. "Patricia, this has been there longer than a few weeks." But Mum was adamant that she had noticed it only a few weeks ago.

"I would like to put a camera up into your nose and then down into your throat to have a proper look," he said.

It was clear that Mum really did not want it done and she was beginning to get upset as the reality began to dawn on her. I was getting upset too but knew I had to keep it together for both of us.

I said reassuringly, "Come on, Mum. We can do this."

The Doctor asked whether he could spray something into her throat to numb it. He then asked if he could put his fingers down her throat. It was the funniest thing ever witnessed, given the circumstances. Mum has hardly any teeth but he did something that caused my Mum discomfort and before we all knew it, Mum made it clear she did not want his fingers down her throat by biting him and pulling him halfway across the room!

The doctor shouted, "Mrs Magee, you are a feisty beggar!"

I couldn't stop laughing and the look on my Mum's and the Doctor's faces was priceless.

After this, we made our way into the other room where the camera would be placed into Mum's nose and then it could go down her throat.   Mum struggled, making a gagging and retching noise. Every time the doctor nearly got a clear shot to get a photograph of what was in Mum's throat, she either pulled away or she made that horrible sound.   Then, out of nowhere, the image was there on the monitor screen.

I saw it and so did the doctor.

The look on his face said everything.   His whole body language told me it was not good news.

My inner voice was saying, "Bollocks...no way... it can't be it ...surely it can't be ...it's her birthday in a few weeks ...please Lord don't let my Mum die."

We went back into Doctor Mahmood's room in silence.

"Ok Patricia, I think you know what I am going to say, don't you?"

People talk about time standing still and, to be honest, I've always thought it a cliché but I swear it felt like the whole of time had stopped. Everything went silent and all I could hear was my heart throbbing in my head. And then he said what I dreaded him saying.

"It's cancer."

I was consumed with the strangest of sensations as if all the blood in my body was draining to the floor. The room began to spin out of control. I looked at my poor Mum, sitting there in her wheelchair. At that moment she looked like an innocent girl, a girl who was lost.

She looked up and said, "I knew you were going to say that."

And then it was as if she went into some kind of shock. She started rambling, fragmented speech, at times lucid but at times not.

"I am not missing my 75th birthday… I lost my one and only daughter… at 39, just three weeks before her 40th birthday… her birthday was a few weeks of being 40 …and my birthday and her birthday are on the same day … 9th of September… I am having my birthday …I am eating at "Old Mother Red Cap" with my son and my grandkids…" Throughout her ramblings, it was clear that we both knew she was going to die but wasn't ready for this.

I couldn't speak. I just sat there thinking about what I was going to say to my children Leona, Mille and Lucas, Mum's grandchildren.

Doctor Mahmood said the tumour had been there longer than the time Mum had stated.

"I think you know what I am going to say. There is nothing we can do. I mean, we could send you to Preston Hospital for radiotherapy, but this will not get rid of the cancer and with your current health I just feel your body would not be able to take the treatment."

The doctor was great, calm and patient with gentleness and kindness that comes with compassion. He said, "Look, let's get some tests done and let's come back in four weeks time. I assure you that you are having your 75th birthday and that your grandkids and John can have a summer holiday. We will take it from there."

We made our way out of the hospital in a state of disbelief. Even though we had both known deep in our hearts that this would be the outcome, the reality of the words being said out loud was somehow unexpected and shocking.

"Right, Mum," I said, "it is like this. We have to be strong for each other and the grandkids. Whatever happens from now on, let's do our best to take one day at a time." Mum nodded mutely.

I helped her tenderly into the car and we got ready to make

the journey home. With my hands resting on the steering wheel and the early summer sunlight streaming through the windscreen, we both knew the journey ahead for us, and all the family was filled with uncertainty.

The Power of Friendship

***

Back at Mum's with a fresh brew in her trembling hands, we sat there. We were both in shock - Stage 4 terminal throat cancer.

"About this summer holiday that you have got booked with Lucas. You are not missing it," Mum insisted. "You've worked hard this year and you need a break, John. Besides, it's not fair on Lucas not having some quality father and son time together. They don't need to see me for another four weeks so I want you going on that holiday."

There she was, once again thinking of the wellbeing of others rather than the fact that she was facing death.

To be honest, it seemed like my head was scrambled – how could I make a decision or even think about a holiday in a time like this? I said, "Mum I really don't know. All I know is we need to get things sorted out for you, what is best for you."

I suggested we call Elaine, Mum's District Nurse. Mum

agreed then asked me if anybody had said how long she had to live.

"If you know, don't tell me. I don't want to know."

What was happening to my world? It had been turned upside down. One minute we were getting on with life and now we had to accept that Mum could be dead within months.

I phoned Elaine and within an hour or two she was round to Mum's place, first to do my Mum's insulin and then to talk about what the hospital had said.

When Mum broke the news to Elaine I could see the sadness overwhelm her. She's been supporting my mum for years. Mum saw her more as a friend than a nurse. The news had broken her heart. Just being in that moment, seeing Elaine and my Mum have that moment together, ripped my heart out. As they both wept, I left the room knowing I had to keep myself together.

When I returned Elaine had regained her composure and was brilliant.

"Right," she said, "listen, we take one day at a time. We are not going to let our minds run away with ourselves. The first thing to do is get onto McMillan and get some sort of care plan in place."

Mum replied calmly, "I'm not going into a hospice. That's

where people go to die."

Elaine wasn't fazed. "Right listen to me, Patricia. We'll have less talk of this death!"

"But I am dying - they told me there is nothing they can do," Mum replied.

And then Elaine explained it – the man crossing the road could have a heart problem for all we know and have a heart attack right there on the spot or the women crossing the road could get knocked over by a car. None of us knows what will happen each day or when we might die. We all have to die.

Here's the thing. We must focus on living for today because at the end of the day that's all we all get, one day at a time. There is no guarantee that tomorrow will come for anyone.

Mum seemed to be calmed by Elaine's words, as though they had given her some peace.

Elaine asked, "Is what you are saying that you want to stay at home?" Mum nodded. "Well, that's fine. You will stay at home and John will take care of you with the grandkids and your family."

Elaine said she would do everything in her power to get the funding so Mum could stay at home.

I was feeling like a dreadful son though still questioning whether I should take Lucas on holiday. It was Elaine that I spoke to. She said, "Look, your Mum isn't going anywhere. You need a break because - when you come back you're going to have a lot on your plate. The break will do you good."

Mum seemed more comfortable so I told her that I was off to meet a friend. It was summer break and I always met my friend Debbie Wright from Avondale Primary school. Debbie and I had worked together last year when I'd been working as a consultant in her school, guiding the teaching staff and kids. We had become firm friends. Knowing it was the summer holidays Mum said she was fine for an hour or two.

I got in my car but it felt like I was in a bubble as I made my way to meet Debbie. We had arranged to have a late lunch. I hadn't told her anything about the lump or that I was at the hospital that morning waiting to get Mum's result. I suppose I'd been hoping that there would be nothing to tell.

I arrived at the pub. Debbie could tell there was something not quite right as I wasn't my normal chirpy self. She gave me a quizzical look as we made our way to the bar. Behind the bar was Sarah, an old friend whom I'd not seen for ages.

"Whatever this good lady would like and a glass of red wine for me - I really need it," I told her with a grim smile.

Debbie and I sat down, a worried look now on her face. I told her the news - about what had happened in the morning, about Mum having throat cancer, about the fact it was terminal and they could not offer any treatment.

What Debbie shared with me then took my breath away. "John," she said," I lost my Mum to cancer a few years ago and it was the most life-transforming experience ever. I miss my Mum every single day. That last part of her journey in this life taught me so much about how precious life is."

Debbie began to tell me that her Mum had been frightened of dying, just like my Mum. Debbie explained, "I told myself I had to grab the bull by the horns and take 100% responsibility. I said to her, 'Right Mother, I want to share something with you. In this last part of your life, I want the time we spend together to be precious, not wasting time on doom and gloom. We will take one day at a time and remember all the good memories. Also, I am going to do something for you. I am going to take you to the door.'"

Debbie's Mum had said "What door?"

Debbie continued. She'd said, "There is a door and I am going to take you to it. when I take you to it Granddad will be there waiting for you. But here's the thing, I can't come through the door with you yet. Only you can go through the door and when it is my time I want you to come and get me.'"

I was mesmerized by Debbie's story, knowing the power of

storytelling through my line of work as it helps others who are going through difficulties in their life. What Debbie shared gave me so much strength – not just the story but having such a good friend with such empathy and understanding.

It was as though she had placed a strong foundation beneath my feet, a foundation that Mum and I could build something on, with the cruel cards that life had just dealt us. Debbie said, "Listen John. You go on that holiday and when you get back you make sure you spend every precious minute of time you can with your Mum. And when the time comes, you take her to the door."

Spain

***

I drove back to Blackburn with some clarity about what I needed to do for the first time. I went straight to Mum's for a heart to heart. The minute I got through the door it was clear Mum had been doing a lot of thinking too.

"How are things going with your work and your Kindness Matters project? Have you shared our news with anyone you are working with? "

"Forget about my work Mum. That can wait and what is going on is between us as a family."

We sat together and talked and I explained that I would take the break with Lucas. Holidays had always been important to us as a family. They were never extravagant but were the basis of such happy memories. I can remember Mum taking me and my best friend John to Blackpool for the day, spoiling us on the Pleasure Beach and eating sugar dummies. One year she and my stepdad, Tommy, saved up and took us all to Pontins at Southport. They were such fond memories of my Mum and Tommy, who'd worked so hard so they could create memories for us. As a family of 11 we had little to go around. I wanted to form similar memories with Lucas, and Mum knew this. In a strange way, Mum also seemed relieved, glad that I was getting on with my life. But I still had a tremendous sense of guilt that I was leaving her when she was so ill.

I'd made the decision to not tell the children how ill Mum was until after the holiday. I didn't want it to spoil Lucas time in the sun. Plus, to be honest, I didn't know where I would find the strength or words to give my children such devastating news.

That week Lucas and I landed in beautiful Murcia to stay at my friend's apartment. The weather was beautiful, not a cloud in sight and the bluest sky I had seen in a long time. Lucas, my son, was so excited. I put on my bravest face and acted as excited as he was but deep inside I was finding it incredibly difficult to get into the holiday vibe.

All I could think about was how Mum must be feeling, knowing she was dying and that she was not going to see me any more or the grandkids, let alone be with them for Christmas. Christmas was so important to Mum, always had been. She loved the decorations, the Christmas tree, and the carols on the radio. Each year we would all go to Old Mother Red Cap, for a traditional Christmas dinner with all the trimmings. It was always her favourite day. She was old fashioned about it, traditional, saving her pension money each week so that she could surprise the grandkids by putting £300 in their cards. I can still see her face light up as she saw their expressions when they opened their cards.

The reality was she was not going to see that and neither were the kids.

I hadn't told the kids that anything was wrong with Mum. I explained to Lucas that if I seemed a little quiet then he wasn't to worry, as I was fine. I just needed some quiet time. However, like most 15-year-olds on holiday, he didn't need his dad's company. He was happy on his iPhone and being in the sun, playing in the pool, meeting new friends.

I did my best to read a book I'd brought on holiday, some best seller with too many twists and turns for a distracted mind, and we chilled out beside the pool. All I could think about was Mum. I knew I had to phone her. When I did she sounded distant, weak and tired, but asked if we were having a good time and how Lucas was getting on. I told her that everything was great, trying to sound as positive as I could. The reality was that all I wanted to say to her was that I was worried sick and that I was coming home to be with her. Though I was surrounded by people having fun, with music and laughter filling the air, I felt completely alone. I felt like I was being torn between two worlds – the world of my dying mother and the world of my growing son. I was somewhere between the two but I felt like I was nowhere at all.

Each day passed quickly and I called Mum often two or three times a day. One day though I said I needed to go for a walk by myself. I knew where I was going and I knew why. I was headed straight to the local bar on the complex. I hadn't had a drink for years, knowing that after the death of my sister and father I'd drank too heavily. Though I had been dry for all that time here I was drinking again. Grief had triggered my drinking in the past and the fact I felt I needed a drink now worried me. In fact, it more than worried me. It really frightened me.

I knew the solution though - every time I felt the need for a drink I had to phone Mum. Hearing her voice would somehow give me the strength I needed despite the almost overwhelming urge to fly back home to her.

I headed back to the apartment and chilled out. I called Mum just to say, "Goodnight, God bless."

Anger

***

The minute I got off the plane I phoned Mum. I couldn't wait to get home and see her. Upon arriving at the house I got through the door and there she was. She had changed so much in such a short period of time as though life was seeping out of her. She was sitting in her usual chair but was somehow more hunched over. There was a great sadness about her. She looked up at me, gave me a half smile and asked how my holiday was. It killed me, seeing her just sitting there in the chair looking so lost.

We chatted about the holiday as though there was nothing wrong. I told her I had wanted to come back and see her every day but had stayed for Lucas's sake. I made Mum a cup of tea and then introduced the idea of what needed to be put in place now that she has chosen to have hospice at home.

As we were talking the front door intercom buzzer rang. It was a woman called Donna from an agency called Kareplus.

They were an independent care company that specialized in the care of the elderly in the end of life care. Suddenly it was all beginning to sink in, to feel very real.

Donna was lovely. She formed an instant rapport with Mum. She explained that the district nurse Elaine had contacted her and told her the situation.

"Pat, I want you to know that we are all here for you."

I suppose I hadn't really thought about how Mum would react but it wasn't how I expected.

"Well, what is the point? I'm dying and that is it," Mum said bluntly.

"Listen Mother. We are all trying to put things in place to make you as comfortable as possible. Can you not see that?"

Before I'd finished my sentence my mum became angry and had a full-blown meltdown.

"Well you're not the one sat in the chair dying are you?" she spat out. "Do you know what it feels like, to know you are dying with cancer? No, you don't! I don't want to die! I don't want to die! I just want to wake up from this bad dream, this fucking nightmare." She looked so full of fury that in that split second the whole atmosphere in the room changed. Although she was so weak she was fighting, trying to get up but couldn't. Donna, one of the carers went to help her but Mum shouted,

"Leave me alone!"

Donna reacted with complete professionalism. "Come on Pat. It's ok to be angry and mad. If you want us to go, we can give you some space. Why don't I pop the kettle on and make you a brew and something to eat?"

Mum's rage continued and I'll admit I didn't handle it well, becoming suddenly so angry myself and saying things that I wish I'd not said. We ended up having a massive argument. I knew that this was doing neither of us any good so I tried to calm down and said, "Listen, Mum, I'm giving you and me some space and I'm going home. I can't cope with this."

Closing the flat door on her, I felt dreadful. I breathed in deeply, trying to think straight. Outside the flat, I phoned Elaine, the district nurse, and left a message for her to call me back. "I've just had a proper meltdown," I said.

My flat was literally across the road from Mum's, an area where the challenges of drugs and crime were all too present. It was where I'd moved to when my mum's health had started to deteriorate 12 months previously, knowing I wanted to take care of her. I walked across the road to my flat feeling like a broken man.

I felt so angry, not just with myself, but with the cancer and everything. Those who know me would describe me as controlled, reserved, positive. But this whole experience had taken over. The whole experience felt somehow surreal as if it was a film I was watching and I had no control over. I couldn't think straight or process the information. I did not know what to do. My inner voice was saying to me, "Right John, come on, you need to be strong." but I didn't have the strength to fight this overwhelming feeling of rage.

As I reached the security door to the flats my phone rang. It was my mate Ray Parker asking if there was anything he could do. The news about Mum's condition was now out there. He suggested that he take me for a walk up in the Lake District to clear my head.

Looking around at the graffiti and inner-city streets surrounding me, the thought of the fresh air, calm and isolation of the Lakes so was tempting. But I also knew that I had to get everything in place for Mum. I thanked him for his kind offer but declined.

I explained, "I just want to get everything in place for Mum. My head is battered, Ray. I'm not sure if I have the strength to do this."

"Listen, John, I'm only a phone call away. You don't need to do this by yourself. Phone me any time, day or night. You're a strong man and your Mum is lucky to have a strong son who is supporting her with this challenge."

As he said that my phone started beeping. It was Elaine, the district nurse, on the other line. I explained to Ray I had to get the call, thanked him for his kindness and that I would be in touch.

I answered the phone. Elaine said, "Right John, let me say this. You're doing a great job and before you say anything else I need you to understand that there's only so much you can do. You are not a nurse or a carer. You are Pat's son."

I listened to her words and knew I could confide in her. "I'm really beginning to suffer from Mum and her cancer. There's so much anger from Mum, from me and others in the family. It's getting me down, burning me out and although I'm trying my best to keep a lid on it, it's still surfacing."

Elaine listened patiently, reassuring me that this was a natural reaction. Elaine also explained that we had had a stroke of luck. She had secured funding for my Mum's End of Life Care Plan. This meant she could have carers in four times a day and we would get three night carers a week. It just meant that somebody else would have to sleep over with Mum for the other four nights.

Without realising the impact or consequences it would have I said, "I will do it."

As I put the phone down and before going into my Mum's flat, I put my hands on the wall and said to myself, "What is going on here? Your head is up your own arse, John. There has to be some light at the end of this very dark tunnel." That's how I ticked - always looking for the positive in any negative situation but this was my Mum. This was terminal cancer. Just the word cancer said it all.

As I stood there, leaning with my hands on that wall, I felt like I was going to collapse or faint. I heard a voice in my head whisper, "Write a book." That voice in my head said, "Write a book about what you and Mum are going through."

Now, to be honest, I wondered whether I was going crazy. They say hearing voices in your head is the first sign of madness. I wondered whether it was still Ray on the phone but the screen was black. I know we all have an inner voice in our heads but this seemed different - this voice was so very peaceful, almost angelic. Strangely, I answered aloud to it.

"Yes," I said.

I went to my phone again and created a folder in Evernote. Without any thought at all, I named the folder Taking her to the door, remembering the words of Debbie and the story of her mother's death.

I walked into Mum's front room and sat down next to her.

There was still tension in the air but I knew I had to put things right.

"Mum, listen. I 've just had a really weird experience. All I know is that it is going to help us with what is going on."

Mum started again, "Yes, but you are not the one dying with cancer."

I knelt down on the floor in front of Mum's chair. I took her hands in mine. "Listen, Mum. I know you are scared. I am scared too but it's no good us getting angry and arguing with each other and saying things we don't mean. I reckon if you and me pull together and take one day at a time, then we will be fine. What do you say?"

She gave a halfhearted, "Yes."

I sat on the chair and then I made the decision. I was going to record the awful experience that we and all our family were going through, in the hope that it could give hope and strength to other families living with terminal cancer.

Grabbing the Bull by the Horns

***

I woke the next morning to the buzzing of my alarm. 5am. I wondered how much sleep I had actually had. However, overnight I had reached a decision – it was time to grab the bull by the horns.

On arriving at Mum's we had a bit of banter as I made her a brew - two tea bags and a drop of milk stirred to the left. I offered her some toast or breakfast but she shook her head – I knew she was already starting to struggle to eat. The tumour in her neck was growing.

I did my best to not let her see my concern with its growth - it was getting obviously bigger by the day.

As I made my way to the front room she asked me, "Is it getting any bigger? It seems as though it is getting bigger, John?"

It killed me to lie to her but I was trying my best not to frighten her.

"I'm not sure," I said. "It looks about the same size to me."

I changed the subject quickly. "Right, Mum, I am on it today! I am going to do my best to start getting things into place for us. We need to get some systems!"

"What do you mean by systems?" Mum asked suspiciously.

"You know...... who is doing what and who is visiting and helping out.... like a rota, Mother!"

It was obvious that Mum wasn't really up for chatting. She seemed locked in her head with her negative thoughts. I knew I had to do something to get her out of that negative headspace. I told her, "I am going to have a chat with Donna from KarePlus - we'll get you some tasty food from Farmfoods."

Hearing this she perked up a bit. "Yes," she said, "I'll have some Holland's meat pies." This made me smile, as she never, ever ate the meat in the pies, only the pastry. It had always tickled the family and me.

Just then, Kirsty, the manager, and Donna from KarePlus came in to do the first visit at 7:30am. I explained that I wanted a detailed plan of who was visiting Mum and taking care of her, the times and which members of staff were doing the days or the night sits. I told them I wanted them to email me on a daily and weekly basis. Mum was insistent that she didn't want any male staff coming or staying over at night as that would make her uncomfortable. That was the last thing I wanted.

Kirsty and Donna were brilliant. They sat down with me and went through a folder. The folder explained how everything was going to work, with the times of who was doing what. Having that clarity helped us all. I explained that it was important for us as a family to know that Mum had as much stability as possible and ideally we needed the same staff taking care of Mum.

They agreed to do their best and that no males would be staying over.

The night sits were still bothering me though. The demands were already having an impact on all of our lives – as a self-employed businessman, the situation was adding increasing pressure on the kids and me. Donna and Kirsty said they would share the three nights between them and the hospice. I said that I'd sleep over on the other nights and see if the kids or any other family members could help me out.

There were other issues to resolve as well. Mum needed much more medication now and we had had issues with our local pharmacy for years – lack of medication for Mum's type 2 diabetes and other health issues.

Just as I was calling them, Elaine, the district nurse, came in. I love this lady so much. She and all her team are brilliant at their jobs. Instantly she was on it. Within minutes she had sorted out a new pharmacy. "They have all the medicine we will need for your Mum's end of life care."

END - OF - LIFE - CARE.

Those words jarred when I heard them and echoed around my head. I knew I had to be strong for Mum, my family and most of all for me, but there it was again, that cold sensation that went from my head to my toes. I knew I had to stay focused and do my best to not cry or break down. But Elaine could see I was putting on a brave face and that the words she had just said had hit me to the core.

"Are you alright, John?" she asked.

I did the old male bravado thing and said that I was fine, but on the inside I was breaking down. I felt numb. In shock. The realisation that my Mum was dying and that her days were numbered was really hitting me hard. I told myself that I had done this for Mum - put all these systems in place with a rota.

If I was struggling to deal with this, what about Mum? Not only was she dealing with her own imminent death but now her home was increasingly full of people she didn't really know.

I could tell that Mum was getting very emotional and overwhelmed with all the people in her flat. Fortunately, Elaine sensed it too and started having a bit of banter with her.

"Come on, Pat. When am I going to get you in that shower so I can wash your bum?!"

Mum and Elaine had this banter going for years as Mum had not been able to get in the shower with her deteriorating health. My Mum loved the banter and would always say to Elaine, "Even my ex-husband never saw my arse so I won't be showing you or anyone else!"

Well, we all started laughing. Elaine kept saying, "Come on, Pat - I've seen it all before and worse than your arse!"

Mum said, "You've not seen my arse though Elaine!" She laughed for the first time in a long time. It helped me, too - seeing this beautiful relationship between Mum and Elaine and how compassionate everyone was towards my Mum, her cancer and her arse!

I started to make phone calls to friends and family explaining that I wanted to get a rota and systems in place. I was concerned that everyone was turning up at the same time and this was distressing Mum and overwhelming her. First up was my Auntie Moo. I love my Auntie Moo as she had always been there for my Mum and me.

My Mum and Auntie Moo had this bizarre relationship since they were little girls. They could have massive arguments and fall out some mornings and then in the evening kiss and make up. Auntie Moo was as regular and reliable as clockwork. She would go into my Mum's flat daily at 7:30am to see if Mum wanted anything from town - and she had done that every day for the last 24 years!

I explained to Auntie Moo that I was going to be telling her other sisters, family and friends that I wanted them to come at set times. She agreed it was a good idea. I never asked her to change her times, as nobody crosses Auntie Moo - I would rather fight ten men than get on the wrong side of her!

That night I stayed at Mum's. She was frightened and she did not want to be alone. I gave the medication to her, which helped her settle. Then I got her into bed and agreed to sleep in the back room. It reminded so much of when my children were tiny babies, or when they were poorly as children - up all through the night checking in on her, responding to any noise or murmur. I didn't get much sleep and I had to be up for work at 5am the next morning. On top of that, I didn't want to let anyone know at work what was going on.

I went to work that day and, I am not joking when I say that it felt as if I was in a bubble. Nothing felt real. I felt disconnected from everything and everyone. I work in various schools as an inspirational speaker and life coach and, although my job is very rewarding and I am seen as a 'Mr. Motivator', at that time

I could have done with someone to motivate me. But I made the decision to pull on all the resources I had and to continue to get all the systems in place for Mum.

On my break, I phoned the hospice and talked about the night sits. I spoke to a lovely lady called Sophie who was the clinical nurse who would check on Mum's situation. She asked if we could put a date in the diary to meet up in the next few weeks. I then phoned all my Mum's sisters - Auntie Rosaline, Olive, Marie - as well as the kids - Leona, Millie and Lucas - to explain that we all had to have set times and agree on who was doing what each day and week.

Even though this was the darkest period in my life I was doing my best to focus on anything positive I could do. Two of my children, Leona and Lucas, were adjusting in their own way to the imminent death of their Nana Pat. Leona lived in Liverpool and agreed that she would take what time she could off work. The baby of the bunch, Lucas, seemed to be taking it hard and did not know how to deal with the news about his beautiful Nana dying. It was also taking so much energy and strength out of me, but I knew that, as long as I could keep looking for the positive in each day, we could get through this together, as a family.

One of the first things that helped me was my other daughter,

Millie. Millie has always been a kind soul but when she started to get involved with helping out I started to see her in a different light. Millie was only 17 years old and was being so supportive and caring for my Mum - she just wanted to take care of her. This made me think that, God forbid, if I were ever in the same situation as my Mum, I know that, without a shadow of a doubt, my Millie would be there to take care of me. It was such a beautiful and maternal side to my daughter which I had never witnessed before shining out of her. She had so much unconditional love and compassion for her Nana Pat. And all of this at such a young age.

Witnessing the interaction between my daughter and my Mum was at times overwhelming. There were times when I had to make an excuse to go to the toilet where I cried my heart out in silence. It was breaking my heart knowing my Mum was dying and my kids were losing their Nana Pat whom they loved so much. When I'd go back into the room I knew they could see I had been crying but they looked at me with that silent acknowledgement. We were all devastated but we had to pull together and be as strong as we could - as a family.

Respect

***

The next day the bed arrived for Mum, meaning that we could finally do our best to get her more comfortable at night, thanks to the funding we'd received from Hospice at Home. I must admit that I felt rather embarrassed and guilty. All this time I had known about the Hospice but I'd never realised that everything was paid for by charity donations. Funding went to help people like my Mum. Time and time again I'd heard of the fantastic care provided by the Hospice but had never considered supporting them and helping them fundraise. The cogs in my brain started to turn.

The delivery guy was really amazing, kind and helpful. He showed us all how to operate the bed. It was like the beds they have in the hospitals that can adjust up and down. If Mum needed bed rest or was struggling getting out of bed then this would help.

Donna and all her team also came to help out with Mum

and get her into the most comfortable position. Mum seemed back to her old self, having us running around like headless chickens, setting up the TV at the bottom of the bed, getting her shopping from Farmfoods, getting her toast and a brew - two tea bags with a drop of milk. Beneath it all though was the feeling that her home was changing. As was she.

After everyone had done what they needed to do and had left the flat, I thought it was a good time to have a bit of a heart to heart - a bit of mother and son time.

Mum's faith had always been strong – brought up as a good Irish Catholic - and, although she rarely attended church now, I knew she still said her prayers, especially in time of need.

I said to Mum, "You know, Mum, I respect you so much and I have an idea. What do you think about this? You know Father Jim from Saint Anne's Church?"

"Yes?" she said.

"Well, I know you say your prayers every day - ," but before I could finish my sentence she had latched on to what I said and started saying, "I never miss my prayers day or night!"

Mum had a table on which were photos of all her family and friends. Pride of place was a photo of my Uncle Robert, whom she missed so dearly, the only boy in the family. Robert had been a strong and lively man, adored by all his sisters. Then one day he went into the hospital for a routine operation. Unfortunately, whilst in hospital he picked up a virus which killed him, devastating the whole family. This experience left a dark shadow in the family, and the slightest mention of the word 'hospital' to his sisters always provokes a shuddering response. So I can understand why Mum thought hospitals and hospices were places you went to die.

She said, "I might not go to church like the rest of our family but I still say my prayers," as she glanced over to the photograph of Uncle Robert.

"What if we invited Father Jim around to anoint you? What do you think?"

Father Jim is our local Priest at Saint Anne's Church and is a bit of a legend in the local community. Everyone who knows him loves him; and besides, he is also Irish, just like Mum. All our family are Irish and Mum has always been so proud of her Irish roots, a place called Kells in County Meath.

I struck whilst the iron was hot and whilst I was at Mum's I called Father Jim. Mum started saying that he'd be too busy and to leave it.

"Ssshhh," I said gently to Mum, "it's ringing."

Father Jim answered the phone with his gentle Irish voice. He was so lovely, already knowing about my Mum's cancer from his parishioners. He told me they had included her in their prayers that Sunday as well as lighting candles for her.

I asked him when he would be able to fit my Mum in for a home visit in order to anoint her. I couldn't believe what he said next. He was already in the local community and could be there in a couple of hours.

I got off the phone and told Mum the good news. She was so happy. It gave her such a boost that her whole body language changed.

"I can't have him see me like this," she said. " I will have to do my hair and put some clean clothes on!"

I helped her into the bedroom and got her some clean clothes out. Mum selected her best skirt and her favourite green top. She always wore green on special occasions or on Saint Patrick's Day. As I was doing this the girls from KarePlus arrived and helped to get Mum freshened up and looking great.

Mum and I sat together and she started to tell me how much it meant to her having her family around and how much she loved her sisters, all of them. It made me feel that I was doing something right for her.

Soon there was a knock at the door. It was Father Jim, a tall well-built man, dark eyes matching his dark hair and beard, and now filling my Mum's small flat with his presence, an overwhelming calmness and gentleness. Love and light entered my Mum's home with Father Jim.

Mum sat in her favourite chair and it was as if I was looking at a little girl. She gazed up and said, "Hello Father Jim."

"Well Pat," Father Jim said. "I wanted to say how honoured I am to come and see you at your beautiful home given the circumstances. I wanted you to know the whole of the Saint Anne's Church are praying for you and that's the reason I am here. I would like to pray with you and John and anoint you in oil."

Father began to pray. My Mum clasped her hands in prayer and was so respectful to Father Jim, it touched my heart. It was as if she was a small girl again at her first Holy Communion. He anointed her head, hands and chest. As he did it Mum seemed to find some sort of peace. He finished the prayers and said, "Pat you will be in my thoughts and prayers and I want you to remember that."

I thanked Father Jim and saw him to the door and thanked him for his time. We both exchanged a look with each other and we both knew that this would be the last time he would ever see my Mum again on this side of the grave.

When I came back into the front room it was as if I was talking to a different person.

"How lovely it is for Father Jim to come out for me. How respectful," she said and then went on to say how much better she now felt. "I know Mum, it was lovely of him," I agreed.

I made Mum a brew and then we began to chat. Mum started to open up to say how much she respected my Auntie Moo and how she regretted some of the nasty things she had said to her over the years during arguments. She didn't want Auntie Moo to regret anything that she had said to Mum and for that to haunt her when Mum was dead. Despite facing death she was still thinking of others.

I explained, "Listen, Mum, we all say things in the heat of the moment. Tell me one person that has never done that and not later regretted it. That's just part of life. I am telling you now Auntie Moo loves you as much as you love her and she will always respect you as you respect her for everything she has done for you."

Mum seemed reassured and then said, "Listen, I want you to do something for me. I have some envelopes and I have written on each one and I am starting with our Muriel."

"What do you mean?" I asked.

She said there was money in each envelope and when she was gone she wanted me to give them to everyone she wanted to leave money for. One of my Mum's key qualities was her kindness. She had always been generous with her time and her money. On this, the final part of her journey on this planet, she was thinking of others as she had always done. Mum had always put others before herself and I guess this is one of the many things I am grateful for in my life. It has definitely rubbed off on me.

That night was going to be her first night sit with the Hospice and I think we were both feeling a little apprehensive. I told her that I would call back later. Despite the apprehension, I was somewhat grateful that someone was sleeping over at Mum's instead of me. It had been taking its toll. I was shattered, juggling work and the kids and I had not slept properly for days on end.

But now it felt like we were making progress. I gave Mum a kiss, said my goodnight and God bless, and gave her a big hug, kissing her tenderly on her forehead. I said I would be back later once I had caught up on some of my work and family stuff.

Each time I left her it was so hard. It's strange but when you're in this position you begin to realise how precious time is. I was beginning to understand the true value of it.

Later that night I returned to Mum's and met Sharon from the Hospice who was there for the night sit. The Hospice staff are so well trained and my Mum was so at ease that I could hear them nattering in the bedroom about the good old days. My ears were on fire and something told me my Mum was dishing out some dirt on me! Given the circumstances, it was lovely to see Mum enjoying the company of the volunteer from the hospice. I gave Mum a kiss good night and did my best not to shed a tear and told her I would be back at 5am the following morning.

I left, looking forward to sleeping in my own bed.

Work-Life Balance

***

The following morning I awoke more rested than I'd felt in ages. I'd had an amazing night's sleep in my own bed and had slept without stirring. I phoned Mum and said I would be over within the hour once I had got things sorted for work.

I knew Mum was worried about me. She thought that my care for her was putting too much pressure on me. She worried about me having an accident whilst driving as I was predominantly doing a lot of work in Blackpool. I thought to myself, "Right, here we go again, let's look for something positive in today."

I arrived at my Mum's and took over the shift from the Hospice nurse until the Kareplus arrived at 7:30am. Mum had had a good night's sleep and some of the meds that Elaine had sorted were clearly helping her calm down and sleep at night. This made both of us feel better.

I explained to Mum that I was going to let everyone know

at work that I needed some time off. Mum was right, my head was not in the right space and I could cause an accident. I gave Mum a kiss and cuddle and we had a bit of banter. Before I left her flat the Kareplus team arrived to help out. I explained to Mum I would phone her throughout the day.

Whilst driving into work, all sorts of thoughts were rushing through my head dominated by the feeling of guilt about taking time off work. I am so passionate about working with young people, encouraging them to stay safe and be decent human beings but I had to be kind to myself for once. I suppose I got it from Mum - putting others before myself.

When I got into Blackpool I went and met with one of my friends who is the headteacher, Stephen Cooke. He is a great head and all the staff at this school are amazing to work with.

Sitting in his office I said, "Stephen I have to tell you something. I am so grateful for the contract I have with you and Unity Academy, but I need some time off. My Mum has terminal cancer." I had been so worried about sharing this situation with work, as I didn't want to come across as unprofessional and uncommitted - I had been working at this school for a number of years and they were as committed to me as I was to them and the pupils.

I was so heartened by his response. "When did this happen,

John?" he asked, the concern showing in both his face and voice.

"About three weeks ago," I explained, " but I didn't want to tell anyone. I felt like I was letting people down."

"Right. It's like this, mate. You take off as much time as you need. Don't even think about work. This is your Mum we are talking about."

To have such understanding and compassion felt like a great weight had been lifted off my shoulders. I thanked Stephen with all my heart for his understanding of this very challenging time in my life.

And the same happened with all the other schools I worked in. They were all so supportive. One of my other friends, Roger Farley, who is the headteacher at Westminster Academy, a primary school in Blackpool, said to me, "It's really important that you talk, John, with friends and family or someone professional, about how you're feeling. We want you to know we're all here for you. I can't believe you didn't say something weeks ago. But the fact of the matter is you are not in this alone. Myself and all the staff will support you and your family the best we can."

I was completely overwhelmed by the kindness of everybody. I spend my working life supporting and helping others, spreading kindness wherever I go but strangely did not expect the same in return. Roger said, "I know you'll be spread thin but, even so, you somehow have to find an hour for yourself. Do your best to switch off." I said I would do my best but that I felt so guilty.

Roger said, "It will be the best thing you can do. Helping yourself personally, in turn, will help your Mum and all the family." He asked me what I enjoyed doing so I told him that I enjoyed walking in nature, the gym, reading, journaling, Yoga etc.

"Perfect," he said. "You find thirty minutes or an hour for your own self-care and I promise you it will help with this horrific thing you are going through with your Mum." Roger had definitely given me some food for thought but I still didn't know how I could fit this self-care in, although I knew I had to give this some thought.

Driving along the motorway on the way back home I started to think about everything that had happened that day - how the response from my colleagues had lifted a massive weight off my shoulder, simply by talking with them. But right then I just wanted to get back and help Mum.

This sense of calm and relief was short-lived. When I walked into Mum's flat she was having a full-on meltdown, stressed, anxious and upset.

" Where have you been?" she shouted.

"I've been at work - you know I have. I called you every hour," I replied as calmly as I could.

"Yes well, it's not you who's dying!" She then started rambling and was talking making no sense, talking mumbo gumbo. It was inevitable I suppose but we ended up having a massive argument. Already feeling vulnerable and stressed, I broke down. I needed my mum – someone to give me the support that she had always given me throughout life but our roles had changed and I was struggling.

"I'm sorry Mum. I can't cope. I'm doing my best but my best just isn't good enough for you right now."

Then it was Mum who broke down. "I am so sorry son but I'm scared of dying. I don't want to die," she cried.

I said, "Come on, us arguing and falling out isn't going to accomplish anything, is it? I am going to phone Elaine. You don't seem your normal self. Maybe the medication to stop the pain and swelling isn't right."

I phoned Elaine and, Elaine, being Elaine, was fantastic. She told me that she would get around on her last call. Elaine arrived and instantly could see Mum was not right. She got onto the chemist and said Mum was not allowed the medication anymore as it had disagreed with her. I asked Elaine if I could speak with her privately whilst the carers took care of Mum.

I was honest with Elaine.

"Elaine, I'm really struggling. I feel like I can't do this anymore. I am doing my best but it's as if Mum doesn't respect what I am doing."

She said, "Stop right there John! I have been in this job for over 15 years and I've never come across a son like you, one that is doing as much as you're doing for their Mother. I'm not just saying that. You're doing a great job but this is what cancer can do to families and great people like you. It breaks them down. You are losing someone you love and you've never been in this position before."

She continued, "Look, you have put all the systems in place with a rota of who is doing what, the care team, hospice at home, the family and friends' visiting times. You have made your Mum as comfortable as she could be. I want you to do something for me. I want you to remind yourself that you are not a carer. You are Pat's son. Do you understand me?"

"Yes," I replied.

"Good. Right, I want you to make time for yourself each day."

I explained to Elaine that this was what Roger had said at

work earlier that day and that I had decided I was not going back into work until the day I was dreading had arrived.

What happened next was truly amazing. Elaine got Mum and me together and said, "Right Pat, I want to help you get out of the bed and sit in your chair. Then you, me and your John are going to have a talk." To Mum, anything Elaine said was like gospel! Elaine and the carers helped Mum walk into the front room using her Zimmer frame and when she'd sat down in her favourite chair Elaine closed the door.

"Right, listen both of you. I need you to both really listen to me. First up, Pat, John is not your carer; he is your son. And John, you are not your Mum's carer - you are her son. Yes, it's hard and we are all struggling to come to terms with the fact that you have cancer but I want you to enjoy being mother and son. Let the care team do what they are here to do. John, I want you to give yourself an hour when they are here and you go for a walk or go to the gym, just something to take your mind off what is going on. Your Mum will be fine, won't you Pat?

Mum agreed and I and Mum kissed and made up. "Besides," said Elaine, "you've got a hospital appointment tomorrow and I don't want you two rolling around the floor knocking ten bells out of each other!"

Mum and I laughed. What would we do without Elaine?

Devastating News

***

The following day Mum and I went to the hospital as arranged. The appointment was for mum to be injected with a dye and then X-rayed, allowing the doctors to see the tumour in more detail. Even before Mum's cancer, the process of getting her to and from the hospital had been a significant challenge – she was riddled with arthritis, had osteoporosis and suffered from type 2 diabetes. It always took a full afternoon getting her in and out of the car and then getting a wheelchair to support her disabilities. On the plus side, we had a disabled badge, which came in handy and enabled us to find parking for when she had hospital or doctor's appointments. Now, with cancer, it was even harder.

Mum was obviously nervous and preoccupied. I said to Mum, "I tell you what, why don't we do lots of random acts of kindness? Only me and you will know."

"Effin' random acts of kindness! What are you like?!" she

smiled.

When we got into the hospital I started paying compliments to people. I have a saying:

A greeting, gesture or a giggle leave other people feeling better than before they met you.

Mum was very well versed on how I operated. After all, I'd been taught by the best!

Mum was always good at putting her sense of humour to it, from her point of view, as I continued to do my random acts of kindness for the members of the public and hospital staff. There was one woman who dropped something and I picked it up. She thanked me for saying that it was very kind of me. Mum's face was priceless.

I said, "See Mum, there you go, a little kindness goes a long way. Did you see that lady's face when I did that act of kindness?"

Mum laughed, "Yes she looked at you like you were after getting into her knickers!"

"Mother!" I said with mock horror.

Mum had always had a wicked sense of humour and this was one of the things I knew I was going to miss so much. Even though we were in this very dark place, I wanted us to have some banter, which would hopefully shine some light on the situation we were in.

When we arrived at the appointment desk the receptionist recognised me from the previous appointment and asked if I was the author who'd donated the Kindness Matters book to the hospital.

I went a little coy and said, "Shhh! Yes…"

But before I could say anything, Mum was full of pride saying, "Yes – he's my son. I was here last time when he left a signed copy of his book." Mum was proud as punch - and so was I.

As we sat down waiting I didn't tell Mum that I'd arranged for my daughter Leona and her partner Freddie to come up from Liverpool for a surprise. My Mum adored her granddaughter Leona and was so super proud of all her achievements, as was I. Within a few minutes, they called for Mum. It was heartbreaking to see how it was such a struggle for Mum to get in and out of the wheelchair and then onto this metal bed so that they could inject Mum with ink in preparation for the X-ray.

The hospital staff were truly fantastic. They explained to Mum that they were going to inject her with ink which would go all around her body and see if the cancer had spread. Mum looked very nervous, as did I, but I said, "Come on Mum, we'll be out of here in no time then I'll take you for a strong brew. Besides I have got a surprise for you when you come out!"

"I bet you have," she said. "What is it? Another random act of bleedin' kindness?"

When I came out my Leona was there. God, I love her. She had brought me a Starbucks' coffee and a slice of cake. She smiled and hugged me but there was sadness in her eyes. Like all of us, I knew she was finding it hard to accept that her Nana Pat was dying. We had a heart to heart then I started to tell her some of the tales Nana Pat had been spinning lately, which made her laugh.

Although Mum was Leona's grandma, she and I had had full custody of Leona since she was a six-month-old baby. Mum's sisters, Muriel and Rosaline, had helped bring her up too; we did it as a family. Tragically, my sister Kathleen, Leona's mother became addicted to heroin soon after Leona was born. This left us no other option than to bring her up ourselves – the alternative would have been for her to go into foster care. Leona is our family and we love her. You could say my Mum became Leona's Mum because that's all she had known since she was a baby. And me, Uncle John, became Daddio.

Just then the nurses and the doctors came out with Mum. When Mum saw Leona her face lit up like the sun on the brightest summer's day. Just seeing the connection between them both really touched my heart.

Mum said, "What are you doing here?" Mum always worried about Leona driving on the motorway. To her, Liverpool was a long way away.

Leona said, "I've come up to spend some time with you. And guess who's in reception?"

Mum pulled a quizzical look. "Freddie!" she said with a beaming smile on her face.

Freddie was Leona's fiancé. Mum had not yet met Freddie, and no doubt poor Freddie was as nervous as my Mum for their first meeting of each other.

When Mum met Freddie, she was fussy and bossy, telling him to get the drinks in and showing Freddie how she was the boss. I could tell my Mum was so happy that Leona was happy and with a lovely boy. It was almost as if Mum felt relieved that Leona was going to be taken care of.

Leona explained that she had spoken with her work employees and was going to get up during the week. Mum, of course, said Leona shouldn't be taking time off work but Leona was having none of it.

Mum said to Freddie, "You're a good looking boy aren't you and you're a big fella too!"

Leona and I looked at each other and started laughing.

"Is that a compliment, Nana Pat?"

I explained to Leona that I would see her later as we had to get back home. The clinical psychologist, the district nurse and a few others had to have a meeting with Mum to discuss the lump and its growth.

When we finally got Mum in the car, Mum suddenly said, "I've been thinking. And, do you know what, I want cremating." I nearly drove the car off the road with the shock. I pulled over quickly.

"What?!" I asked.

She continued, "In fact I want you to drive me to the crematorium now. I'll show you where I want to be. I want to be in the same section of the crematorium so I can be next to our Kathleen and Robert."

I started the car up again and we made our way to the crematorium. Whilst we were driving there she continued, "I want you to spread my ashes with my brother and some in Ireland. I want my remembrance stone to be near my daughter Kathleen." Mum had never got over the devastating loss of my sister, dying at the age of 39 due to substance misuse. The ironic thing was my Mum and my sister had the same birth date, the 9th of September.

As we got there Mum said, "That is where I want to be, with my daughter and my brother." Although it is a Catholic tradition to be buried I respected my Mum's wishes, as my sister also had been cremated. I knew that Mum was preparing herself for her death and it seemed to give her a sense of peace yet to me it was devastating.

When we were back at Mum's flat it wasn't long before the intercom buzzer sounded with the arrival of the Hospice staff and the district nurses. Mum started to panic and was so stressed, saying, "I mean it, John, if they tell you how long I have got left, I do not want to know." It was starting again, this overwhelming emotion and fear. I had to be strong for Mum. She didn't want to hear the prognosis.

Mum was a little more settled so we left her in the front room with one of the hospice staff as we went into the back room. Elaine's boss and Sophie from the hospice were there. They began by saying how well my Mum was doing and then moved on to what had happened at the hospital. To be honest, with the visit of Leona and the trip to the crematorium, the outcome of the hospital had drifted to the back of my mind.

"Listen John. What I am about to say might sound overwhelming and frightening, but we are looking at the worst-case scenario. The tumour is growing at a rapid rate and we are concerned that it could explode. We would like you to buy some red or burgundy towels for the worst-case scenario of blood…"

What?! I was dumbstruck.

They assured me that this might not happen but it was needed as a precaution. With Mum being at home it was a possibility. They said, "Look, John, it's not looking good. The tumour is very aggressive and growing very quickly. We do not want your Mum to be in any more discomfort so I am suggesting a syringe driver, which will inject morphine when your Mum is in pain. It will help with the pain."

I couldn't believe what I was hearing. It was all starting to move so quickly.

In shock, my voice trembling, and my heart beating ever so fast, I asked, "But she will make it for Christmas, won't she?"

The room was silent. No one replied.

Sophie looked at me and it was as if Time stopped. "Listen, John. We are all doing our best for your Mum. What I would say is that you need to let all your Mum's direct family know there's not long left."

I was desperate for more time. "How long are we talking? A month? Two months?

"Maybe only two weeks."

The words shook me to the core. I felt numb, speechless, frozen. I heard Elaine say, "John you'll be alright. We will all take care of your Mum."

All I was thinking was how could the time have gone so quickly? How could I go to the front room and say nothing to Mum? How could I not let her see it in my face?

I went into the front room with Elaine. She knew that Mum had asked not to know what they had told me. It killed me not telling her the truth but she had asked for that and I wanted to respect her wishes.

"Mum, they told me what we have to do to stop the pain and get you more comfortable. That's right Elaine, isn't it?"

"Yes," said Elaine with a gentle smile. "Right, Pat, what we are going to do is get a syringe driver in place. That's morphine, which will help with any pain. Also, it will help you sleep a bit better."

I felt in complete turmoil. A part of me just wanted her to live and be healthy but another part of me wanted to stop her suffering so much. I felt so awful knowing that a part of me wanted her to die in peace.

My head was absolutely battered, as was my Mum's.

We got Mum comfortable and then I told Mum that I would need to have a chat with all the family. I knew that the conversations were going to be the hardest ones in my life.

Taking Her to the Door

***

I walked out into the cool night air, hoping that the change of environment would give me the strength to make the phone calls I had to make. Auntie Moo had to be first as head of the family. She was the one who pulled all the strings, keeping us together and in place. I have so much respect for her as she has always been like a second mother to Kathleen and me when we were growing up. She was also always there for my Mum in the bad times. Growing up on the council estate things were challenging at times but Auntie Moo was always there to support us.

"Auntie Moo," I said, "the specialist has been… we have had a meeting …" I spoke haltingly, struggling to get the words out.

"Go on then, what have they said?"

I just couldn't do it. I couldn't get the words out. It was as if there was a hand on my windpipe, squeezing it tightly. I just couldn't talk.

"What is it, John? Tell me."

In a choked voice I said, "It's best I come round and see you. I don't want this over the phone. I want to do this face to face."

"Surely it's not that bad?" she asked.

"I'm on my way," I muttered and put the phone down.

My heart was breaking, knowing what my Auntie Moo and all Mum's sisters were going through. The news I was going to give them would devastate them even more. Why did we all have to go through pain? And then there was my poor Mum, waiting to die and living on borrowed time.

I pressed the intercom buzzer and auntie Moo answered.

We went through our usual routine - a little bit of normality in the middle of a nightmare.

"It's your favourite nephew," I said and she said, "Who? George?!"

I thought, even in these darkest of moments we still have to shine some light.

When I got into Auntie Moo's flat I couldn't even look at her, let alone speak.

Reassuringly, she said, "Go on, son, what have they said? Has she got until after Christmas? Will the tumour stop growing? Will she be in less pain?" So many questions, all asking for hope when I had none to give her.

"Auntie Moo," I said, "It's not good. I need you to do something for me and my Mum."

"Anything," she said, "What?"

"I need you to get onto our Rosaline, Olive and Marie, all my aunties, all my Mum's sisters and family and let them know that it may only be a couple of weeks ..."

"A couple of weeks? What? Are you joking? What?" She crumpled before me, the cornerstone of the family, crushed and broken. Then she started crying, my Auntie Moo, and talking in a fragmented way about the horror of losing her sister. It was too awful to see.

I stood there thinking about why cancer has to affect so many people in such a devastating way. Surely there has to be something positive that can come out of the horrible situation we are all in. At that moment I could see nothing but darkness.

I left my auntie's flat feeling broken and emotionally exhausted. Knowing Auntie Moo would round up all the family, I made my way back to Mum's, which was only around the corner from my Auntie Moo and Auntie Rosaline. Like many working class families, they had thrived living so close to each other.

By the time I got back to Mum's flat, I knew I had to make these final few weeks the best they could possibly be. I decided

I would ask Mum what she wanted. Inside the flat all the carers who were there greeted me. I perched on the end of Mum's bed and said, "Right what do you want me to do?"

Mum loved asking me to do things for her, "Can you put my TV higher at the bottom of the bed and see if you can find Columbo or Midsummer Murders." She loved her TV did Mum.

"No problem," I replied with a loving smile.

It was clear from the look in her eyes she was still frightened and did not like it if I left, even if it was for 15 minutes.

"Right, listen, I need to have a chat with you when these lot have cleared off."

"What about?" she asked curiously.

"I'll tell you in a bit," I smiled.

Once the carers had gone it gave us a couple of hours together to have some quality time to talk - before the hospice staff returned for the night sit.

That was when I told my mum Debbie's story about her mother's death.

"One of my good friends, Debbie, shared a lovely story with me about when she took care of her mum with cancer. She told her mum a story which had given her hope and strength. It was a story about taking her to the door and we are going to do the same."

Mum said, "I don't get what you mean?"

I continued, "We are both frightened, right? Yes! We are both very sad about what we are going through, agreed? Yes! And we both don't know what the next stage of this journey is. So, I'm going to suggest taking you to the door."

As I was describing this story to my Mum I looked over her shoulder as if I was looking at a door. She looked behind her and said, "What feckin' door?"

"Mum, you are so funny! It's a metaphor. I believe it's what's going to happen to you. You have always said how much you miss Kathleen. I promise you this, I am going to take you to this door and at the last bit of this journey you will see a door with light and I promise you our Kathleen is going to come and collect you."

Her little face sort of lit up. I then said to her, holding her hand, "And Mum, when my time comes to pass, I want you to promise you'll come and collect me when my kids take me to the door."

Mum said, squeezing my hand gently, "Of course I will."

There was a peacefulness as me and Mum sat in this quietness, each in deep contemplation of what was coming next, as we prepared to take her to the door.

As we sat there, I remembered a conversation I had with a

friend, Dave Green, about the unconditional love our mothers give us. He'd said at the time, "John, do you have any idea what you would have put your Mum through whilst you were in her stomach for nine months?" He'd asked me if I had ever thanked my Mum for carrying me for nine months?

I looked at my mum and said, "Mum I want to thank you for carrying me in your stomach for nine months."

"Yes, well you were an awkward little sod as well. I had to have a Caesarean section with you. You've always been an awkward bugger," she laughed.

"I want to thank you, Mum, for never giving up on me when I was up to no good as a lad and being in trouble with the police, getting involved in crime and drugs."

She replied, "You're my son. I would never give up on you."

"Have I been a good son, mum? Have I made you proud?" I asked.

Mum then did something she had never done before. She asked me to help her sit up in bed. I used the electronics remote control and did my best to help her sit at the end of the bed.

She sat there looking and picking at her nails and looking down at her knees. She always did this when she was gathering in her feelings. She looked like a little girl in her nightgown and fluffy slippers, head gazing down and picking her nails. I knew she also did this when she was worried or feeling emotional. She then gazed up at me and said, "I need to tell you something. I am so proud that you wrote your book 'Kindness Matters'. My son, an author. You know I was only messing when I was slating you and the book to the carers?"

I felt such a lump rising in my throat and then she looked down again and it went silent again.

She picked her nails and clasped her hands together looked up at me and said, "Do you know something? The next book you write will be better than the last one you wrote..."

It felt as though my heart was being wrenched out of my chest and even now, as I am writing this, it blows me away. Mum had no idea that I was keeping a journal and making notes to help with the daily pain I was going through. I knew these notes would become this book, written to give families who are going through cancer hope and strength. It was totally surreal, like an epiphany.

Mum then began telling me how proud she was of the grandkids and that, when I had taken her to the door, to make sure that they all got their envelopes with their cash inside and that Auntie Moo and all her sisters had an envelope each, apart from Auntie Rosaline who would get two envelopes, as she was Mum's favourite - the baby of the bunch.

The Power of Storytelling

***

That evening the buzzer went on the intercom. It was Auntie Rosie. She had been coming over every night like clockwork, sitting in the bedroom with Mum and talking about the good old days, sharing stories of their childhood. This got me thinking about the power of storytelling.

When I am doing my job as a life coach or giving motivational talks to kids, the well-crafted stories I tell them to help them associate with positive feelings from memory. With this in mind I said, "Come on, tell us a tale, Auntie Roz, what you remember of Nana Pat?" - we all referred to her as Nana Pat, even me. Auntie Rosie pulled a corker out of the top drawer and said to Mum, "Do you remember when I was about five years old and you bought me that teddy bear called BoBo?"

My Mum exclaimed, "What? That's nearly sixty years ago? How would I remember that?"

"Well," said my Auntie Rosie, "I still have that teddy on my bed and it has slept with me every night for the last sixty years since you bought it for me. In fact, he is looking a bit more worn and torn than me!"

Mum and Rosie began to laugh. My Mum's face was priceless. Seeing her look so happy filled me with so much pleasure even though I knew this joy would not last long. Auntie Rosie still lived in my Grandma and Grandad's house, the house that my Mum grew up in when they landed here in the UK as Irish immigrants. It had a place in all of our hearts and was only across the way from my Mum's flat.

Auntie Rosie said, "I tell you what Pat, I will bring BoBo across to see you tomorrow night."

I said, "Are you sure, Roz?"

Well, Mum started chuntering on. "Listen, you do as you're told!"

"Oh, here we go again! Auntie Rosie the golden child and John is the big bad wolf!" I laughed.

"Come on. Why don't we all share some stories?"

I wanted to do this to take Mum's mind off any negative thoughts that were going through her mind.

Auntie Roz said, 'Why don't you tell your John that story of when you went to Blackpool with that man when you were kids and John's Dad found out."

Suddenly my Mum began laughing with a full heart and so did Rosie.

"Come on, spill the beans. What's the craic?"

Mum started her story. "Me and your dad had a break up from courting and one of my friends, Michael, offered to take me to Blackpool for the day. When your Dad found out he went mad and looked for the guy and gave him a beating. The thing was after your dad had given him a beating he got the news that the guy Michael was gay. He was batting for the other side," she laughed. "Your dad was so embarrassed he went and apologized for his jealousy and his actions."

Mum then began telling us stories how my dad and his friend John Cliff would try and get her and her friend in the long grass, so they could try and have their wicked way! My Mum and Rosie were laughing like schoolgirls. They would say, "But we're Irish Catholics and we don't do that sort of thing until we are married!"

Mum then started to share with us all the many fond memories she had from staying with her family in Ireland in Kells, County Meath. She loved going to the Cross of Kells and visiting the river and bridge on Maudlin Road. She was so proud of her Irish roots. She told us how our claim to fame was that the actress Maureen O'Hara was related to our Granny.

Mum had loved being out in the countryside and remembered how friendly everyone was.

The buzzer interrupted our stories. This time it was a very pleasant surprise. After her divorce from my father, my Mum had a relationship with my stepdad Tommy, whom she loved and missed dearly. Now some of my stepbrothers and sisters had come to see her. It was Thomas, Michaela, Jean and Lizzie. My Mum was as happy as a pig in muck! They too started telling stories about the good old days – days of drinking and singing all the Irish songs in the Manxman Pub and Centurion Pub and how my Mum's friend Auntie Alice, who was Tommy's sister, was an amazing singer. The sharing of those moments, those stories is something I will treasure for the rest of my life.

It was now getting late, so, slowly but surely, everyone started to go, leaving just me and my Auntie Rosie. As the flat quietened the atmosphere changed. I could tell that Mum was beginning to get upset again. I gave her medicine to calm her down and knew that it would be tomorrow that the syringe driver was going to be put in. Mum then started getting angry and taking it out on me. I said, "Come on now, it's important that you take your medicine."

"Well I'm the one dying!" she moaned.

I said, "I told you every time you say that we are going to put a pound in the jar!" I thought to myself, 'I am going to do my best to still have a sense of humour with Mum.'

Auntie Rosie was watching it all like a live performance.

I laid Mum down gently, the pain now etched on her face and got her comfy with her pillows. I then proceeded to take one of the pillows and said, "Ok, are you comfortable? Nothing to see here," and I pretended to put the pillow over her head like I was suffocating her. Well, the smiles and laughter returned. She then kept trying to flick water over me by putting her fingers in her cup of water. This became our game. We all loved it and it was our way of finding some fun and a little light in this very dark place.

I then began telling them jokes. I said, "I know what we will do. Next time we get you out in the wheelchair and I am taking you around the block, you can lift your skirt and flash at the taxi drivers that drive through town. We all know you don't wear any knickers! Can you imagine the look on the taxi driver's face. It would be like his birthday, Christmas and Eid all came at once. I guarantee he would be scarred for life and would take that image to the grave!" Well me, Rosie and Mum had tears rolling down our faces and laughed until our sides ached. Mum said, "I will do it, you know. In fact, I could do with some fresh air!"

After we had all had our laughter and fun it was time for Auntie Rosie to leave and for the Hospice staff to help me. As I got my Mum settled I gave her the medication before bed and then gave her a kiss on the head. As I got ready to go home I realized I'd have only a handful of hours of sleep and then I'd be back up and at it again at 5am. I was beginning to learn to live in the moment and take each of these moments as they came. The systems and rota were all in place but I was under no illusion that everything could change in the blink of an eye.

A Celebrity Visit

***

The minute I awoke there was a voicemail from Elaine saying she would be round first thing that morning to fit the syringe driver. My stomach tightened and once again I was instantly overwhelmed by emotion. I knew I had to pull myself together for Mum and all the family. I had to do everything in my power not to reveal to Mum that I was on the edge of breaking down completely. I had to find the resilience to do this, but it was so hard.

I went to Mum's and did my morning routine. I asked if she had slept well. She had a good moan saying she'd had no sleep but how great the Hospice nurse was. She said she'd been up all night and she had only had a few hours' sleep. Mum never sleeps a lot and usually would be up at 2:30 am or 3 am in the morning. She did like a nap in the chair during the day though!

The buzzer went at the door, and it was Elaine and Sadie the district nurses. They had brought a safe for the morphine and the syringe driver. Mum looked really worried but Elaine being Elaine soon helped my Mum feel at ease. To see Elaine's kindness to my Mum always touched my heart. Her care and compassion were heartwarming. She asked my Mum if it was ok if I went to sit in the front room while she fitted the machine. Once it had been fitted she came in to explain the safety aspects of having morphine in the flat, and the dangers. She showed me how to put it in the safe and to let all the Hospice and carers know where it was, but it was me that had to take care of it.

Elaine explained that she had to get to her next appointment, but she would be back after dinner. As I saw her out my phone began ringing. I wondered who could be ringing at such an early hour. When I realized who it was, I couldn't believe it – it was the international best selling writer and inspirational speaker, Richard McCann. I told Mum I need to take the call and that I wouldn't be long.

I met Richard back in 2009 when he'd given me my first big break at the beginning of my inspirational speaking events. I'd spoken on the BBC with him at an event in Leeds called "A way out" which was funded by Yorkshire Police. It was designed to show reoffending drug users that they could break their addiction, with the right support and time, which would be put in through various rehabilitation programmes.

Richard said, "Hi John. Please forgive me but I had just seen your news about your Mum on Facebook. I am gutted for you, mate. I know you always said that your Mum is a big fan of my books and work and, if it is alright with you, I would like to come and meet your Mum in person to read to her my new book called Just a Man. I understand if you want your privacy at this time, I just felt I had to ask."

I couldn't believe it - this man is recognized as one of the top 10 speakers in the world. Richard' s story is inspirational and from it comes his 'I Can' attitude. His story is about how his Mum was the first victim of the serial killer Peter Sutcliffe who became known as 'The Yorkshire Ripper'. He shares the story of the horrific ordeal he and his family went through, the awful consequences of one man's actions of taking his mother's life in such a barbaric way.

Mum had read his other books, *Just a Boy* and *The Boy Grows Up* and she had loved them. I had even got them signed by Richard, and now this guy was offering to take time out of his busy schedule to come and see my Mum. I could not believe his kindness.

"When do you think you could come?" I asked.

"Listen, Johnny, if I can, I'll come today. I'll cancel all my speaking events and would be honoured to read to your Mother and have a brew and a biscuit."

"Deal," I said.

"Great - I will speak to my PA Tracy and move all my talks for today. See you in the next couple of hours."

I could not believe it. I ran back into the bedroom and said, "Mum, Mum I've got a surprise for you!" Although she wanted to know I said, "I'm going to keep you in suspense but, trust me, you're going to thank me for this."

Before I knew it the buzzer of the intercom sounded. And there was Richard McCann standing in my mum's flat. He looked fantastic with his smart waistcoat, shirt and tie. He was also wearing the nicest shoes I'd ever seen.

"Right, how do you want to do this?" he asked.

"Wait there and I will go into the bedroom and say to Mum that her surprise is here."

I went in - Mum was looking weaker every day - but then I said to her, "Guess who's come to see you?"

Just then Richard walked into the bedroom. My Mum's eyes nearly popped out of her head and then she began to go all coy and shy like a young girl meeting her crush. I said, "You know who this is, don't you?"

"Of course I do, you prick!" Good old Mum - she always had a funny way of showing me how she loved me.

Richard began to laugh and then sat down to chat with my Mum. Richard, being Richard, said, "Are you going to get the kettle on? And don't forget the biscuits." He may have been wearing some very nice shoes but you could tell he'd grown up on a council estate like us, not frightened of asking. I went and made him a cuppa' and didn't forget the biscuits.

When I went back into the bedroom Richard had helped my Mum out of her bed to sit at the bottom end of the bed. He said, "Pat I have a gift for you. I have brought down my new book, which was only released a couple of weeks ago called 'Just a Man'. I'd like to read you the introduction and share with you what I've written in the book. It's about how, after my Mum passed away and when my sister Sonia committed suicide, I started to notice the number 44. My belief is that my Mum and sister were connecting to me from the other side. Now I am not into any of this but in my book, I put the puzzle together and it gives us all hope that our loved ones are always with us, that they have ways of communicating with us. One of the ways they do this is through electrical items."

I couldn't believe it. What Richard was saying was a miracle, an amazing coincidence or synchronicity. Mum's greatest fear was death; you could see it in her face. She told me she didn't want to die, that she was scared, and here was one of my Mum's favourite celebrities and authors, sitting in her bedroom, talking to her but most of all giving her the hope and strength. She did not need to be frightened of death. Death was just a doorway.

Richard began by reading the introduction to my Mum and then went onto the first chapter. Mum and I were engrossed. I could tell from the outset that this was going to help Mum so much. Richard stopped reading and then had a chat about his experiences and said, "Listen Pat, I am not sitting where you are but I promise you, there is nothing to be frightened of." Mum then told Richard about the analogy 'taking her to the door' and how she had accepted what I'd said. She had now begun to accept the idea.

Richard then said, "Listen, John, I want you to do something for me. I want you to read to your Mum every night and let me know how you get on." I agreed, saying it would be a pleasure and that I thought Mum would love it. Richard said he had to get back home. He gave my Mum a hug and kiss and thanked me for the brew and biscuits. I could tell from the sincere look in his eye that he knew he would never see or speak to Mum again.

Then again, I was beginning to realise that the time was getting closer for all of us, and soon we too would not be able to speak or see my Mum anymore.

Dignity

***

The next day Mum's health started to deteriorate rapidly. Even though we knew she was dying the aggression of the cancer was still shocking. It was ravaging her body and each day she was becoming weaker to the extent that she struggled to get out of bed. She was as weak as a kitten. I kept saying, "Come on Mum, you can do it."

Mum started to cry, "I can't John, I just can't." I did my best to hold back the tears but I couldn't. We wept together.

I said, "Come on Mum, we have to get you on the commode."

I struggled so much to move her and all the time she was really desperate for the bathroom. The carers were not due for another hour and I knew I had to get her there. It was like lifting a dead weight and at times I felt I didn't have the strength no matter what I tried to do. Even using the slide sheet it seemed futile. Mum was getting more and more desperate for the toilet and started to lose her temper. She began screaming at me.

With one almighty effort, I made a sharp jerk to pull Mum up and get her to the commode. She let out an almighty scream.

Devastated I said, "I'm sorry Mum, I didn't mean to hurt you."

"It's my back! It's my back! I can't move," she cried. Mum had damaged her back years ago – three broken vertebrae. I knew that we may have done some really serious damage. I knew that I shouldn't try to move her again but there she was, semi-naked, in pain, stuck on the commode and in the midst of having a poo. This was my mum – there was no dignity here. It was killing me.

I kept saying to myself, 'John how many nappies has your Mum cleaned off you?' but it was so hard. I wasn't built for this but I knew I had to do it. This was my Mum. We were both sobbing. "Where are the carers? We don't need this, Mum," I said.

She just sobbed, unable to move, stuck on the commode with her morphine not working. I begged Mum to bear with me.

I called Elaine and the carers and said, "I need help! Mum has hurt her back and she is semi-naked and stuck on the commode and I don't know what to do." I felt so helpless.

Thankfully the buzzer went and it was Donna, the carer, and Elaine. They took over instantly and asked me to sit in the front room. I broke down and I thought. 'I can't do this anymore but I have got to. It's my Mum for crying out loud.'

Elaine came in the front room and spoke to me.

"John you're doing an amazing job. I've never met a son like you that has done so much for their mum in this situation."

"But why do I feel like I'm doing a rubbish job?" I gasped.

"Listen to me, you're doing a fantastic job and your Mum is very grateful, as are we all. But the bad news is, John, it's not good. Your Mum's back is bad and it's not looking good. I know you said you'd spoken with your family about the hospice. What did they say?"

I explained that we had all agreed that if it got any worse we wanted Mum's well-being to be of paramount importance.

"But," I said, "Mum is frightened to death of going to the hospice. She thinks if she goes in she won't be coming back out."

Elaine asked if she and Mum could have a private conversation. "Of course", I agreed.

While Elaine was in the bedroom I tried to pull on every emotional resource I had. I kept repeating affirmations in my head.

"Peace is the result of accepting life as it is rather than how you think it could be"

"This shall soon pass"

Affirmations were one of the only things I could do that were giving me some sanity.

Elaine shouted for me to come into the bedroom. Mum looked dreadful, racked with pain and so pale and weak. Elaine said, "I've had a bit of a chat with your Mum and she has agreed to go into the hospice for some respite care. I have explained there is a waiting list but we will do whatever we can.

I said to Mum, "Are you sure?" She nodded in agreement. "Look, we'll get you as comfortable as possible, I promise."

Elaine explained that we would need to up the morphine and also get some additional medication for the pain.

I looked at Mum. It was as if she was fading away before my eyes. The next thing Mum had to have a catheter fitted, which she was not happy about, but it was the only way as we could no longer get her out of bed. I wondered how much more pain she'd have to go through. When will this stop?

The buzzer went. It was my daughter Millie. There was no way I wanted Millie to see her Nana Pat the way she was at that time. She loved her Nana Pat so much, often staying over at Mum's. They would get into bed together, cuddle up with teddy bears and Mum would make Millie laugh with her funny stories. Now it had come to this.

I spoke with Millie and said, "Listen, Millie, it's not looking good. We all have to be incredibly strong for Nana Pat and stay as positive as we can. We've agreed for her to go into the hospice but we are waiting for a bed."

Millie asked, "But she is going to be here for Christmas isn't she, Dad?"

I didn't reply for a few seconds but it was enough for her to understand.

"Listen. All we have to do is take one day at a time. You go and get the kettle on and I'll sort all this stuff out with the nurses."

Just as I said that I began to get an increased awareness that our time together, with Mum, was getting very short. It was out of all of our hands now. All we could do was to accept the situation and continue to do our best.

Choices

***

The thought of making the choice for Mum to go into the hospice was one that I had been dreading but thankfully Mum had made the choice herself.   Deep down I knew it was the right decision – in the hospice, she would get around the clock care that she clearly now needed. Thinking back, since Mum's cancer diagnosis, I had been faced with so many choices all of which I had found difficult.   I started to affirm and tell myself, 'I am doing my best until I find a better way of handling situations.'

Mum and I were chatting in her bedroom. She was so very weak by this stage. However, she was still bothered about her family getting their envelopes. "Promise me you will give all those envelopes out." Rosaline, who would get two envelopes, was Mum's favourite as the baby of the bunch; then there was Marie, Olive, Auntie Moo - she was grateful for all Auntie Moo did for her - Pat upstairs, George her neighbour, Leona, Millie and Lucas. It was heart-wrenching how my Mum, despite being in so much pain, was still thinking of others with her kindness.

The phone went and it was the hospice. A bed had become available and they were ready to take Mum. Within what seemed like no time at all an ambulance arrived with paramedics. Mum, however, still couldn't move because of the pain and her back. The paramedics had to use the slide sheets to get her out of bed but still, she screamed the house down in pain. It was a truly awful time. I began to cry, I just couldn't hold back the tears. Eventually, we got her in the ambulance. The paramedics were brilliant, so patient and considerate.

In the ambulance, they asked me for Mum's date of birth and address to confirm her identity. It all seemed surreal as Mum lay there, groaning in pain. While they were driving the paramedic said, "Listen, Patricia, we will go as slow as we can but there are a lot of bumps because we are in a residential area." Just as he said this we hit a speed bump. Mum shouted out, "Póg mo hole!" (translates as 'Kiss my ass hole!').

"That's an interesting phrase. What language? I've never heard that before. What is it?"

I explained, "Mum was speaking Gaelic but it's best you don't know what she said!"

Mum started laughing through her pain and so did I. Then

she started counting in Gaelic and saying her prayers in Gaelic. It was a moment with very mixed emotions as if she was returning to her childhood in Ireland.

We finally arrived at the hospice. The staff were fantastic and they gave us a room that was like a 5-star room at the Hilton - Mum had an ensuite bathroom with her own TV, bed, chairs, and they said all the family could come and go as they pleased. They got Mum comfortable and Liz the Doctor was amazing, not to mention all the staff who were very professional and helpful, making Mum and all our family feel at ease.

Once they'd got Mum settled in her room I came out of the room thinking I could do with a strong cup of tea. The nurses offered to make me refreshments and said, "John, if you or your family want some quiet time there is a quiet room and some lovely gardens to go and get some fresh air. Take a walk, if you want." So I took advantage of the tea and the gardens and I went out to clear my head.

Little did I know that those last prayers in Gaelic in the ambulance would be the final words I ever heard Mum say. I would never hear her voice again. I will never take for granted the words of a loved one.

I built up the courage and phoned all the family, telling them that Mum was now in the hospice and that she was comfortable.

I told them that we could come and go as we wanted, staying as long as we wanted to. Almost before I could even put down the phone my Auntie Moo arrived at the hospice. She looked distraught and I could tell she was finding it hard seeing her sister like this. Then again so were we all.

Without a doubt, we had made the right choice for Mum's well-being and her final days on earth. It became so hard for us all and, even though Mum did not want to die in the hospice, we all wanted to do what was best for her overall well-being. Mum and all of us felt the deeply compassionate support from the hospice staff.

As I was comforting Mum, Elaine the district nurse came into the room. Elaine was much more than Mum's nurse, she was my Mum's friend. The compassion and care etched into her face nearly broke me. The love she had for Mum was incredible and we were so grateful for it. She loved my Mum, we all did, and we all knew that the time was getting closer. The woman we all loved was getting ready for her transition. I was trying to prepare myself mentally and emotionally, thinking about what was coming next, preparing myself for what we had agreed on - to take her to the door.

But I was frightened.

Family

***

Even in the darkest of places, there is light.

In this situation, it was the overwhelming love and care of Mum's family. We knew that we were all in it together and it was truly wonderful to have all of my Mum's family at this dreadful time. All of her sisters were there, my cousins, the grandchildren, all gathered around the bed, sharing stories of the good old days and reminiscing about some of the funny things Mum had done. She had once made my dad a pie out of dog food after he had rolled in drunk having spent what remained of the weekly budget on beer, rather than food for the kids.

There were times when Pat or Moo or any one of us would come to help out. Mum would sit in her favourite chair - or what I called 'Mission Control' because she would have us doing everything for her - then the minute you went out of the door she would start slagging you off, saying how we'd always get her shopping list wrong. We all knew that mum could be a bit two-faced but that was just how she was.

"I asked for boiled ham and I got roast ham," she'd say or, "She always forgets my receipt! Who forgets to get a receipt?"

We all began to laugh at these stories and in a weird way I could tell Mum was listening to all of us.

We could feel the love from everyone but the situation itself was overwhelming for my Mum's sisters. They washed her face, kept hugging her and talking to her with so much love and respect. I knew that the love in the room was like nothing I had ever experienced before and probably would never experience again. These were grown women, mothers themselves, but they were more like young girls who share and care for each other. There was such an outpouring of their sisterly love in a way I had never seen from them before. They loved their sister Pat and just wanted to make her as comfortable as possible in these final moments, as did everyone else.

I told the family that I wanted to sleep over at the hospice. I was happy to sleep on the settee, knowing I couldn't and wouldn't leave my Mum alone. The little time I had left was so very precious and I wanted all of it. I wanted to take her to the door as we had agreed, to take her to my sister Kathleen who would collect her.

The family was worried that they may not be there when mum passed and so they were reluctant to leave. I assured them that I would let them know immediately if Mum started to deteriorate, so that Mum and I were left alone.

I stayed at the hospice that night and held Mum's hand all night. I went into the deepest sleep ever. I had not slept properly for weeks, always on edge expecting to be woken up by bad news, and I was shattered. I suppose that within me there was a sense of relief that Mum was receiving excellent care in the hospice, meaning that I didn't have to worry as much.

Before I knew it, it was morning and all the family were back in the room.

Soon, Mum started to make a strange and dreadful sound.

The doctor came and asked to speak to me. "There is not long now."

The nurse took me quietly to the side and gently said, "Please don't be frightened of the noise – it's what happens." The noise was the death rattle – when the body is shutting down and some functions like swallowing, stop working. She reassured me that Mum was not in any pain and that the noise, although disturbing, was more distressing for those hearing it than the person dying.

Auntie Marie suggested that we all gather around the bed to

touch Mum and comfort her. Then we started to pray:

> *Hail Mary,*
> *Full of Grace,*
> *The Lord is with thee.*
> *Blessed art thou among women,*
> *and blessed is the fruit*
> *of thy womb, Jesus.*
> *Holy Mary,*
> *Mother of God,*
> *pray for us sinners now,*
> *and at the hour of our death.*

All my family surrounded her - my Mum's sisters, grandkids and cousins. I have never experienced such an outpouring of love like that in my life. We encircled her bed, hugging and stroking my Mum's hair, touching her hands. She was being enveloped in our love. It truly was a beautiful and unique experience despite it being so very sad. I felt like I was in a dream.

In turn, we started thanking Mum for everything - for the good times, the laughs, the arguments, the things we had said and done. Soon some began to weep and then we all began to cry together, some sobbing, some moaning with grief while some of us began to wale. It was so emotional and draining but it was ok; we were all expressing our own individual love for this beautiful human being, my Mum, Nana Pat, Auntie Pat, a sister to Rosaline, Muriel, Olive, Marie and Robert.

I said to Mum, "It's ok Mum, you can go to the door like we talked about. Kathleen is waiting for you."

But Mum wasn't ready yet or just did not want to go. We finished our prayers and dried our tears and looked at Mum laid there on the bed, helpless but clinging on to life.

Leona said, "Do you think she is waiting for Nena the cat to come or is it for Millie to come?" Then Millie arrived but Mum kept hanging in there. She was not ready to go to the door just yet.

Angel Number 44

***

Millie's arrival totally changed the energy in the room; it was as if Mum had waited for Millie to be there. It was strange how we all sensed it and knew the time had almost come.

My Auntie Rosaline asked, "John, did you finish reading the book that Richard McCann gave you to read to your Mum?" I nodded at her. "I'd like to read it if you've finished as it sounded interesting, especially the bit about life after death."

As Auntie Rosie passed me the book I realized there was an extra chapter, an epilogue, so I said, "Look there is an extra chapter."

Auntie Rosie suggested, "Why don't you read it out loud for us all to hear, John."

I began reading from Just a Man and all the family fell silent and listened along with Mum. The epilogue detailed how Richard felt he had been contacted or connected to his Mum and his sister through the number 44. He also wrote about the music that was personal to him. When I had finished reading it we had a really good discussion about whether Richard was just looking for signs of 44 or 4 or, like he said at the end of the book, signs of 22 or 33.

We all agreed that there are many questions which cannot be answered and besides, if it gives people comfort, then for me that is good enough.

A hush fell on the room again as we waited. As I looked around the room a strange experience began to unfold. All the family seemed to be on their phones. It didn't bother me that they were on their devices, it was just that I had said I wouldn't use my phone in the hospice unless it was really needed.

As I gazed across the bed at my Auntie Rosaline I continued to hold my Mum's hand. "Rosaline, will you pass me my phone please?"

As she passed it over to me I nearly dropped it on the floor.

"What is it?" she asked.

One of the folders on my iPhone had the number 44 on it. I said, "Look, everyone. Nana Pat is playing games!" showing the phone screen to the family. There were a few nervous giggles but I had to admit I thought it was a bizarre coincidence. I continued, "I know what! Why don't I look on Google and see what Angel Number 44 means?" Richard had mentioned

Doreen Virtue's Angel Numbers. I typed the words into the phone and up it came. I read out loud in a clear voice:

"The Angels are giving you extra comfort, love and support right now. Ask them for help with everything, and listen to their guidance through your intuition."

As I finished reading the quotation aloud, a peaceful silence entered the room like none of us had experienced before. We looked at each other as if to say, 'Can you feel that peace and stillness?' There were no words. Time stood still in that moment as we all looked at Mum and realised that she had taken herself to the door.

Soon we began to cry. We said our goodbyes to her, thanking Mum for all the amazing memories, for her love and kindness. The nurse quietly came into the room. As she did, I glanced at the clock. 22:44. The nurse checked Mum's pulse then said to us all, "Pat is at peace now." She recorded the time of death as 22:44.

Gradually the rest of the family drifted away, each to grieve and remember in their own way. I stayed with my Mum, not wanting to leave her. I thanked her for everything she had done for me, making me the man I have become. I made promises to her - the things I wanted to achieve in memory of her, like releasing more books and making November the official

Kindness Month in every UK school by taking my Kindness Matters 30 Day Challenge.

I knew I needed to leave but I couldn't. I stayed, stroking her face and holding her hand. Soon the colour faded from her cheeks and warmth left her body. I stood up to go then gave her one last hug and a few last words.

I told myself, "John you are a good son. You did your Mum proud. You promised her you would take her to the door and you have done. She is with Kathleen and the rest of your family. Now it's time to take care of the rest of the family on this side of the door."

Funeral Arrangements

***

I went back to Mum's flat. When I entered it was still filled with the familiar smell of my mum but it felt so quiet, empty and lonely. Looking around, I half expected to hear her voice saying "Where have you been, John? I've left you voicemails. I wanted you to go to the chippy for me." At that moment I would have done anything to hear her right then, giving me a telling off.

I stood and looked around the room and thought of all the memories and moments we had shared in this flat. Years and years we had been here but now I knew I would never again ask her if she wanted her brew with two tea bags and that drop of milk.

I sat on the sofa, feeling numb, looking at her empty chair. There was still the imprint in the cushion from when she had last sat there. I looked at all her family pictures on the wall, on the fireplace and mantlepiece across from her table. Her very own altar of my Granny, Uncle Robert, Dennis and so many other family and friends that she had lost and that she prayed for every day.

I smiled when I saw Mum's mobility scooter. She had never used it but my Mum's cat, Nena, who made a favourite resting place out of it, loved it. That cat had a life of luxury, sitting on a £2000 scooter! All that was just a memory now.

I turned off all the lights one by one, apart from the one in the front room and landing. I didn't want the flat to be in darkness – it would all seem a bit final. I made my way home feeling empty inside and still not quite believing that Mum had really gone.

The following day I awoke to a phone call from Darren at Oswaldtwistle Funerals. I already knew Darren from when my sister and Dad had died years before. He had proved to be a good friend at the time and beyond. However, hearing his voice now this was starting to bring back all that grief and made me realize that from that childhood family of four, there was only me left now. I had to be strong though.

Darren's professional approach made me feel a little better. He assured me that he would take very good care of Mum and that he'd manage all the funeral arrangements through me. Any special requests I had, he would sort out. I explained to

Darren that, when Mum was first diagnosed, she'd made the decision to be cremated despite being christened a Catholic. She had also asked to have her remembrance stone near my sister. Darren told me that some families don't discuss those arrangements beforehand and it can lead to all sorts of arguments at what is already a very difficult time. Because Mum and I had this conversation, it made the funeral plan very straightforward. I remembered organising my sister's and my Dad's funerals, being advised by some close friends that, if you're in a position to discuss your loved one's dying wishes with them, then it helps with the funeral process and helps the rest of the family respect these wishes.

Despite knowing what Mum wanted and having it clear in my head, the process of discussing it with someone else was an ordeal. I was overwhelmed with a sense of loss, flooded with the grief I'd experienced at each death. I had to do my best to stay focused. I kept on practising different affirmations that helped me with my pain. Two, in particular, were helpful:

'Peace is the result of accepting things as they are rather than how I think they could be'

Whenever thoughts and emotions were replaying inside of me I remembered the Ho'oponopono affirmation, 'I'm sorry, please forgive me, thank you, I love you'.

Repeating these silently helped massively. Every time I found myself disappearing inside my head, having regrets or feeling emotional, I would repeat these and other affirmations.

Darren asked if there were any other special arrangements. I explained that I wanted bagpipes to be played and for all donations to be made to East Lancashire Hospice. Also to have some Irish songs that were mine and my Mum's favourites, ones we would sing in the house or when I would take her out in the car. As sad as it was Mum and I did really well, talking about her dying wishes, and this, in a funny kind of way, made the funeral plans a little easier.

I called my Auntie Moo and explained what had been arranged and asked if she or any of my Mum's sisters had special requests. She explained Auntie Marie and some of the other family wanted to organise some beautiful flowers for my Mum and that they'd decided on green, white and gold. Even in this horrible situation, coming together as a family like this really touched my heart. Growing up I'd always felt like a bit of a lone ranger but now I was feeling the love of my family like I had never felt before.

I asked Auntie Moo whether she could help with the list of things that needed doing such as food, flowers, music, phone calls, the order of service etc. She was already on it with Marie,

Olive, Rosaline and all my cousins and family. This took a massive weight off my shoulders.

But I knew that the next hardest part was yet to come - the funeral and, finally, the letting go.

The Funeral

***

The day had arrived. It was a beautiful sunny day, the sky the clearest of blues. It felt as though Mum was there with us all. It was a day I had been dreading, knowing I would be overcome with emotion. On the other hand, it was the time for us all to let go of the person we all loved - my Mum, Nana Pat, a friend to many, including me. I had told myself and all the family, as sad as we all were, we had to do our best to make the funeral a celebration of Mum's life, of what we had gained rather than what we had lost.

We all had gathered at my Dad's old council flat where I was living, as it was just across the road from my Mum's flat. I put the kettle on and did my best to make everybody welcome although the atmosphere was tense and sombre.

It was great to see my Uncle Noel, the cousins and other family relatives that I'd not seen in a year. Inside of me there was so much pain but I just wanted to keep it together the best

I could for my kids Leona, Millie and Lucas. They were all heartbroken. I held them close and told them how proud Mum was of them all. I told them that Mum wouldn't want us all upset and, as hard as it was for us, to have a good cry but to remember the good times and all the good memories.

I said to the kids, "What do you think she'd be saying now?" and some of my Mum's one-liners came out - 'Yeah, well you never do anything for me anyway!'

Then Leona said, "What about 'Why don't you go and please yourself - you always do anyway!'"

Then Lucas and Millie said, "Let's not forget, 'Yeah well!!!'"

We laughed loudly together, remembering the strength of her character and personality or some of the funny habits she had; and, believe me, she had a few.

Then Darren arrived in the limousine and a hush descended on the room. As always Darren was in fine form, stopping all of the traffic on the road so we could get into the car. As the car slowly made its way to Saint Anne's Church, the kids found it too hard not to cry. I did my best to keep it together but soon we were all crying together, with our hearts broken, thinking about the amazing lady who was no longer in our lives.

I tried to lighten the mood and said "Remember what your Nana Pat used to say: 'You never do anything for me anyway.

Why don't you go please yourself, you always do anyway!'
Well, she'd be impressed today!" Mum swore like a trooper,
even in the most serious of situations. Then Millie mentioned
her Holland's meat pies that she would take all the meat out of
before only eating the pastry. We began to laugh with tears of
joy.

The happiness was short-lived though. As we got to the
church the melancholic sound of bagpipes rang through the air
and the sense of occasion hit us all hard. I was overwhelmed,
thinking of my Dad's funeral, Kathleen's and so many other
lost friends and family. My hands started to shake and my
mouth went dry.

As I got out of the car I glimpsed friends and family I'd not
seen for a long time - my old school and lifelong friend Lee
Duffy, my good friend Fergal, who had arranged to carry the
coffin with me, and my cousins, David and Patrick.

Darren placed the Irish flag on my Mum's coffin and Fergal,
Patrick, David and I prepared ourselves to carry her into the
church. I felt like I was going to faint. I felt lightheaded and
unsteady. The only thing that was keeping me on my feet was
the support I felt by the number of friends and family that had
come to the funeral.

Father Paul had agreed to take the service and he was

amazing. The service opened with one of Mum's favourite hymns, 'I watch the sunrise', then Father Paul spoke to the congregation about how my Mum was well respected and known in the community. I know that church isn't for everyone but every word he said and how described my Mum was heartwarming. My cousins Denise, Bernadette and Sarah gave readings. Mum would have been so proud of how well they did. Then the moment came when Father Paul invited me up to give the eulogy.

I had been doing well until he mentioned my name. Suddenly I felt overwhelmed again. I walked to the front of the church and as I looked up there all I could see was a sea of bodies in front of me. I opened my mouth but no words came out. I felt as if there was no wind in me.

Father Paul seemed to be by my side straight away with a glass of water and kind words of encouragement, "Take as much time as you need, John."

I looked down and said to myself, "This is for you Mum. Please tell me what to say." Then I looked and began by telling some of the funny things we all knew about my Mum, such as cursing and swearing like a trooper; and her funny eating habits such as a McDonald's quarter pounder with nothing on the bun except the burger; or her version of a Chinese takeaway

- fried rice with no onions. The whole church began to laugh. I shared with them all that Mum did not want anyone attending today to be upset, that she wanted them to celebrate her life. Soon the moment came and I read out the words I had written to describe her 'My Beautiful Mother'.

FROM MY EULOGY

Thank you, Mum, for carrying me in your womb for nine months

Thank you, Mum, for feeding and clothing me

Thank you, Mum, for changing my nappies

Thank you, Mum, for bathing me and keeping me warm

Thank you, Mum, for teaching me how to walk and talk

Thank you, Mum, for keeping me safe

Thank you, Mum, for teaching me the difference between right and wrong

Thank you, Mum, for never giving up on me

Thank you, Mum, for always believing in me (especially when I did not believe in myself)

Thank you, Mum, for always having time for me

Thank you, Mum, for showing me the meaning of kindness

Thank you, Mum, for all the fantastic memories

Thank you, Mum, for being you.

When I finished there wasn't a dry eye in the church.

Everybody clapped and cheered - I had done it; I had made my Mum proud.

We made our way outside with the coffin and onwards to the crematorium. We all sat in the limousine in silence, each of us sobbing and holding each other. No words could take away the pain that we were feeling. We all knew that we were getting ever so closer to saying our very last goodbye to the kindest lady we all knew and who had shaped our lives in so many ways. When we arrived at the crematorium the bagpipes were playing again.

When we entered the crematorium chapel, I was greeted by my Mum's cousins from Ireland whom I'd never met before - Dee, Fiona and Brenda. As we sat down the music started playing. It was an Irish song by the Wolfe Tones, My heart is in Ireland. It was a favourite of my Mum's, and all the cousins and family started to sing it. The experience was incredible, so moving and so full of love. Then the moment came when Father Paul delivered his final prayers for my Mum, the curtains closed and we all left the crematorium in tears.

It was over. Strangely, I felt lighter, that there was a kind of peace settling.

We headed to 'The Redcap' for the wake. It was where my Mum loved to go for food. When I got there I couldn't believe it. Claudia, Tracy, Kenny, Dave Green and so many other friends who are part of my 'Kindness Matters' online community were there waiting. They paid their respects and said the funeral had been a wonderful tribute to my Mum. The Guinness started to flow as everyone had a different story to tell about Mum. Even though the alcohol was easing my emotions I knew it would be so easy to fall into the same trap as I did when I'd lost my sister and my father. I was mindful that this time I had to keep control.

After a few hours, we knew that it was time to go. We all hugged and gave our respects to each other. Taxis were ordered and, one by one, the group dwindled. As it became quieter I had that feeling that I needed to be alone, to go back to the flat and reflect and accept everything that had happened that day.

The Aftermath

***

I woke up the following day with the worst hangover ever. The minute I made my way to the kitchen, I heard my critical self-talk saying, "I thought you don't drink anymore?" The minute I heard that I began with an affirmation and said to myself 'My thoughts are balanced and supportive. My decisions support my peace of mind.' The affirmation was right but what I really needed now was some paracetamol!

I picked up my phone and saw there was a lovely message from a girl called Demi. She was a friend of a friend that I'd met a couple of times. She'd sent me the most beautiful message offering her condolences. We had already talked about meeting up before Mum became ill, as she was keen to talk about my Kindness Matters project and how it could tie into what she was doing with her Reiki. I replied to the message and asked what her availability was to meet up. We agreed to meet up the following day at The Sanctuary of Healing.

The following day Demi and I met up and the minute we met there was an almost electric connection between us. As she sat down in the room, I said, "Do you feel that?" It was like a surge of energy had hit me in my stomach. Demi said she felt the same thing too. We went and had lunch and we were like two cackling hens, talking about how we both love to support and work with people who are going through trauma or life challenges.

Demi said, "Listen, John, I'd like to give you a free Reiki treatment. I feel it will help you massively after what you have just been through, taking care of your Mum and the whole funeral arrangement. Why don't we strike while the iron's hot? Shall we go to my place now?"

I thought to myself, 'What's the worst that can happen?' And besides, I really needed some TLC. We arrived at Lotus Healing in Darwen which is where Demi and her friend Katy do their Reiki Healing. Even though I'd heard people talk about Reiki and had countless people who were master practitioners, I had never really experienced it.

Demi asked me to take off my shoes and made me feel very comfortable. Then she put on a lovely song quietly, called '100,000 Angels' by a group called Bliss. It felt like every word they sang was describing Mum.

I had my eyes closed and felt the most blissful experience. I felt like I had gone from all this heartache to experiencing release and healing all from this lovely and kindhearted woman.

The next thing I knew Demi was saying, "John, when you are ready, you can come into the other room and put your shoes on. There is a glass of water waiting for you."

What had just happened? I felt incredible, with an overwhelming feeling of joy and happiness running through my whole body. It was as though all the negative thoughts had floated away out of my head. I didn't fully understand what had happened or how, but I felt so much better for it.

Upon entering the other room, Demi said, "John, I am a big fan of what you do but in my opinion, I think you need some time to adjust your energy. You give a lot of energy to people, and now it is time for you to give some back to yourself."

As a typical male, I said, "I'll be alright - I've been through this before with my sister and dad and I know the process." The thing was, I didn't realise at the time how very wrong I was. I didn't know where this grief would take me.

I thanked Demi for her kindness and made my way home. However, as soon as I entered my flat my mood changed and I went straight into the kitchen for a drink. Opening the fridge I pulled out some cans of Wainwrights and drank them quickly and without thought. I then had some Two Hoots, a traditional ale from Manchester which I love. That, too, went down so well. The cold refreshing taste and feel of the ale took the edge off the negative thoughts I was having at the time. I knew what I was doing and I knew that this would become a problem. In a strange but predictable way I convinced myself that it was helping me to relax and, as when my sister and Dad died, I decided to keep the drinking to myself and not tell anyone.

The phone rang and it was Father Barry. Father Barry was the priest who'd buried my sister and dad. He is an amazing man, a tower of strength. He offered me his condolences and said, "I know it is a bit short notice but I'd like to take you for something to eat. Can we meet later for dinner?"

I said, "Because it is you, Father Barry, why not?"

We met at The Fernhurst pub where it was great to see Father Barry. The thing about him is that he doesn't pull any punches or mince his words. Within five minutes he said to me, "John you look careworn."

Not being familiar with the phrase I asked, "What's that?"

"There is an old adage - 'The worst-dressed man in town is the tailor'."

Still, I didn't understand. He explained that, with my being a public speaker and an author helping people with my kindness,

I'd forgotten about myself. He strongly advised me to take the time to grieve.

Then, out of the blue, he just said it. "I don't believe that you've grieved properly for your sister or dad yet, have you?"

I was speechless. Then I said to him, "I think you're right." I told Father Barry that I had got a taste for the drink and he put me in my place. We both had so much common ground - he is of Irish descent and he had experienced alcoholism in the family when he was a child. Also, when he'd been a prison padre he'd buried hundreds of young people who'd died too young from alcohol and substance misuse.

"Listen to me, John," he said. "We both know the consequences of alcohol. It will not do you any favours. It's a depressant. In fact, it will do you more harm than good."

I agreed with him and said, "If I feel it is getting out of hand I will call you."

We finished the meal, ordered the taxis and we both went our separate ways. As I sat in the back of the taxi I began to reflect on the two main things that had come up after the funeral - Reiki with Demi and alcohol. I said to myself, 'You are going to have to make a choice.'

The Wall

***

The following morning when I awoke I received so many messages of support and the one message that struck me was the one from Demi. I instantly started my day with her on Facebook Messenger and we talked about how we had so many things in common. Then she opened up to me about when her grandmother had died and the impact it had had on her life. She also told me about the work she does with her Reiki.

I questioned what was going on. I had just begun the journey of grief and this lovely lady had come into my life. The thing was, I wasn't looking for a relationship; however, I knew, and could tell that I liked Demi, and something was telling me that she liked me too.

After I had finished talking to Demi I began to feel a real sense of sadness. I sat myself down and began to journal my feelings.

Over the years journaling has been my lifesaver, helping me

reflect on the times in my life when I have needed to change. I wrote in my journal about my drinking as well as my awareness of what I was doing and why. I also wrote in my journal that, if I felt like it was getting out of hand, I would talk to a member of the family or speak with a counsellor.

As I finished my entry, I sat in silence in my apartment. I knew at that moment what had begun to happen to me. I was experiencing grief. Over the years I had gained my qualifications in NLP, which is a form of counselling, and I had learnt some therapy called The Bereavement Curve. It helps the client understand the stage they are at in their grief and, even though I have life-coached people with grief, this was a different kettle of fish. This was me.

I opened up my MacBook and found the diagram *(see page 174) As I looked at the bereavement curve I could quite easily identify where I was. I was in the stage of guilt and sadness, and what I was doing to cope with my guilt and sadness was masking it by drinking alcohol in the house, alone, and not telling anyone. I started going through my head and saying:

- Was it my fault that Mum died?
- Could I have done more?
- Where was this self-doubt coming from?

I went to the fridge, got a beer and drank it in one. And

then I got another one. Even though I knew what I was doing to myself, the drinking was masking the pain of my emotions and my developing mental health issues. I sat down again and looked at the bereavement curve and I still tried to justify to myself that I was not in that stage of my grief. I said to myself, 'Come on John, pull yourself together. There is always a solution, and the solution is that you need to talk to someone because it is getting out of hand.'

Despite this, I had this overwhelming urge not to tell anyone, not even my cousin Lee, with whom I usually shared everything, especially when my head was all over the place.

I sat in the apartment all day and turned off my phone. I just wanted to be alone.

As I sat there in silence feeling numb and separate from the rest of the world, I heard a voice say, "Phone your Sarah." Sarah is a close cousin, like a sister to me and she is an amazing counsellor. Her nickname is 'Mash' based on her love of mashed potatoes!

I switched my phone back on and nervously dialled her number. She picked up the phone immediately and, as we talked, I could hear the concern in her voice. I knew she was concerned for my well-being and I also knew I could tell Mash anything. Her calm voice was filled with so much compassion.

I thanked her for her support at the funeral and then I opened up to her about what I was going through. "Listen," I said, "I know a lot of men struggle with mental health. I am drinking again and I know I'm being stubborn. The Hospice has offered me six counselling and holistic treatment sessions as part of the grieving process but I've not taken them up on the offer." I explained that I was justifying not going by saying that I am a trained life coach and I could - and should - be able to get through this alone.

Sarah was brilliant. She got me switched on straight away. She said, "Listen, those sessions cost £60 each, so that's £720 worth of valuable help waiting for you. Besides, if you don't like it, what have you lost?"

I told Sarah about meeting Demi and how she had come into my life at just the right time and, even though I was not looking for a relationship, she was helping me feel good despite the situation.

Sarah listened then said, "I want you to do something for me. I really want you to step outside your comfort zone and go and have the counselling and the holistic treatment from the hospice. It would mean a lot to me." I love my cousin Sarah so much and I told her I would call them in the morning.

I went to sleep wondering about what the next day would bring.

Depression

***

The following morning I woke up remembering what Sarah had said. But I could hear the critical self-talk kicking in - 'It's pathetic that you need a counsellor? You're an NLP trainer. What would all those people you've coached think of you? You know what is going on here without being told. You've been through this before with your sister and your dad and countless friends - how can this experience be any different?'

How wrong could I be? And all this was down to the fact that I was drinking again.

I also remembered the conversation with Father Barry - that I needed to take care of myself; that, in helping others, I was constantly putting them before my own well-being; that I was in need of some self-loving kindness. Although I kept repeating my affirmations, I had this heavy feeling in my stomach, a feeling that I just didn't want to speak to anyone.

Looking at the screen of my phone, I had messages from

colleagues at work, my kids, family friends, and a message from Demi. I didn't want to speak to any of them. I turned off my phone and I sat with the pain all day. I meditated, said prayers of thanks for my Mum's life, wrote in my journal, repeated affirmations all day but still, I didn't want to speak to anybody.

The days passed and still I hadn't replied to messages or called anyone. Then I received a message from Demi - she told me that she wanted to come and see me. I really didn't want to see anyone but something inside me said to let her come around. I desperately wanted to tell her how low I was feeling, what I was saying and doing to myself behind closed doors. But I also knew the only person that was going to get me through this transition was me. The first step was that I needed to talk to someone.

Demi arrived with her big smile and bubbly personality. She is such a beautiful soul.

"Get that kettle on," she smiled. A proper Darwen lass.

Demi made me feel better and I really wanted to tell her what was going on. However deep inside me, I felt I couldn't burden her with my grief. She suggested we go for a walk sometime later that week - she knew a lovely place and she said that it would do me the world of good. I said I'd give it some thought, explaining to her that I'd some personal stuff I was working on and that I needed to be alone.

She gave me so much empathy and compassion and was so understanding. As she stood up to leave we cuddled each other. It felt so good, to have that warmth and affection, and then before I knew it we began to kiss. All the pain disappeared in that moment. I quickly came to my senses and apologised for overstepping the mark.

Demi said, "Don't apologise – I really like you, John. You're a good, kind soul and I want you to know that if you need me, call any time. But I know you need space and I'll give you that. I do understand what you are going through."

Who was this girl? It felt like she was an angel, sent in disguise to rescue me from the hell that I had been through in the last sixth months.

When Demi left I went onto Google and typed in 'signs of depression'. The first site that came up was The Samaritans. It listed the telltale signs of depression.

- Down, upset or tearful
- Guilty, worthless and self-critical
- Empty and numb
- Avoiding social events and activities you usually enjoy
- Using more tobacco, alcohol or other drugs than usual
- Solitude

The list went on. Everything on the website described exactly how I had been feeling. This grief was nothing like what I'd experienced with my sister or my Dad. Could Father Barry be right when he'd said about me not grieving for my sister and dad? Now I was experiencing the grief for all three at once.

I knew I had to reach a decision. I went and meditated. While I sat there I used a technique I had learnt from the late great Louise Hay. You say to yourself, 'What is it I need to know?'

What is it I need to know? Sure enough, the answer came later on - I heard my inner voice telling me to phone the hospice and accept the counselling and holistic treatment. Acting on this, I went into the front room and phoned the hospice. As usual, the staff were wonderful and they arranged an appointment for me the following Friday.

Somehow I knew that this would do me more good than harm.

Counselling and Reiki

***

It was a new year, January 2019, a year I had hoped would be the best year to date. Just like the rest of the world, I had to get back into the swing of things but it was dark in the morning, dark at 4pm and cold and dismal in between. Then gloomy days were darkening my mood but something inside said, 'Come on John remember what cousin Sarah said'. So I made a conscious decision to go for my first appointment for my counselling and the holistic treatment at the hospice.

Despite the decision to move forward, I could still hear the critical self-talk in my head - 'You're a man. You don't need counselling. You're a life coach. You know what's going on... ' and even though I was aware of what I was saying to myself I also knew I had to be open to these opportunities and possibilities. What was the worst that could happen? Besides, I needed to practice what I preach when I am coaching people. I often talk about the critical self-talk and about some of the things we say to ourselves, how we can be our own worst enemy and how saying positive affirmations can help with unhelpful self-talk.

I wondered about how I would react to returning to the hospice. Would all those unhappy memories come flooding back? As I entered the hospice, it was surreal. The strange thing was that I didn't feel as sad. What did upset me though was seeing other people who were either coming to comfort a loved one or who were suffering with cancer themselves.

The staff, who are mainly volunteers, were absolutely amazing. They made me feel so welcome. I was seated in a reception area, brought a glass of water and told that Karen would be with me in 5 minutes. As I sat there, I started an affirmation 'My thoughts are balanced and supportive. My decisions support my peace of mind.' I kept repeating this affirmation inside my head, and, whilst doing so, I heard a woman's voice say, "Johnny? Hi!"

As I looked around I saw Bev - who was my friend and the wife of my old boxing coach. Bev always had such a happy and chirpy personality, always immaculately turned out - a really vivacious woman. However, on this occasion, she was very different and I felt a profound sadness from her. Bev told me she had lost all her hair but that it was now growing back. It looked like she had also lost an awful lot of weight. She told me that she had been diagnosed with breast cancer in the autumn. She had had a double mastectomy along with chemotherapy and radiotherapy. It had knocked her sideways so she had been coming to the hospice for treatment, including Reiki and counselling, which had done her so much good.

I was delighted that she'd said that, as it made me feel much more at ease. She said, "Johnny, you will love it here. The way they make you feel is incredible."

I only touched on briefly what I had gone through with Mum, as I did not want to frighten Bev. I said, "I'll get in touch with your Baz. It would be good to have a catch-up."

And then on that, the receptionist said, "John Magee? Karen is ready to see you."

I gave Bev a big hug and told her that she would be in my thoughts and prayers.

I have to admit that, when I met Karen the counsellor, I felt very odd but I remembered what my cousin Sarah had said about it. It would help me and, if it didn't, it hadn't cost me any money - which is always a bonus!

Karen was lovely. She had a beautiful way of listening to me with empathy and, before I knew it, I was telling her all about my life, not just what had happened with Mum. It was whilst talking with her that I explained to her what happened not long after I had received the news about Mum having terminal cancer, where I'd been outside her apartment and heard a voice say, 'write a book'. I'd honestly thought the voice had come from my phone because I had just had a conversation with my friend Ray but I had heard that voice over the years and I just put it down to that inner voice which we all have to keep us safe.

Karen was amazing. She said, "I really believe you heard what you heard. You're not going crazy."

Well, that was a bonus to hear! Then I began to explain that I had started writing and putting a book together and had called it Taking Her to the Door – the day cancer came knocking. I also said that I wanted to do a fundraiser and give all proceeds to the Hospice as a 'thank you' for everything they'd done for Mum and my family, and for the great work they were doing to help people like me get counselling and other alternative holistic treatments.

Karen explained that, although it was fitting for me to do what I was doing, I still had to find time to grieve. I opened up to her about knowing the model, the bereavement curve, and I explained that I was a qualified NLP life coach.

Karen explained, "I get that John but it's different when you are going through grief yourself. What I would encourage you to do is to have more self-care for yourself. What do you enjoy doing as well as your writing?"

I told her that I like to walk in the countryside, cook good food, journal, meditate and read. She said, "That's wonderful." I told her that I had missed the countryside and that my girlfriend had suggested a lovely walk. Karen said, "That would be perfect," and before I knew it the hour was up. Karen arranged for me to see her the same time a week later and said, "Enjoy your treatment with your therapist, Ashleigh."

I left the room feeling incredible. Despite having spent years counselling, I'd never been on the receiving end and hadn't realised just how powerful and helpful counselling was. I sat in the hall and before I knew it a lovely lady called Ashleigh came to get me. She had a calm, gentle voice with a lovely energy about her, and she brought me to a small room where she explained that she could do reflexology with me. I explained that I didn't need reflexology, as my friend Sheila Nelson takes care of me every other month, which I find really helpful when I'm feeling pressure from work or life in general. Ashleigh explained that they also did massage and Reiki - I thought it strange that Reiki kept coming up.

I explained to Ashleigh that my girlfriend was a Reiki Master and she kindly asked who my girlfriend was. When I told her it was Demi she said, "Yes, I've heard of her - she is a very good Reiki healer. On that note, would you like some Reiki?"

Once I had got on the bed I felt something that I had never felt before. It was like a release. The next thing I knew I could hear Ashleigh saying, "You can get up when you are ready now, John. There is a glass of water there for you." I had been asleep for 30 minutes and something magical had happened but I didn't know what.

Ashleigh suggested making the appointments an hour before or after I was seeing Karen, which fitted perfectly. We set up our next appointment, and I left the hospice, knowing that what had happened had been a life-changing experience from both Karen and Ashleigh.

Self-Care

***

The following day I began to reflect on my experience of the counselling with Karen and the Reiki with Ashleigh, and on how, in that one session, there had been a lifting of some of the depression. The whole experience had such a positive impact. Even though it had only been a few months since Mum had died, the treatment was so helpful for my overall emotional well-being.

I received a message from Demi asking if we could go on the walk she had planned. At that moment the feelings of anxiety and depression began to grow again - it was as if I felt guilty for wanting to go out and enjoy myself. At that moment, I just wanted to stay at home and be left alone. However, I remembered what Karen had said about needing to do those things that I classed as my self-care.

I love nature. I really do, and I was really enjoying being in Demi's company. She would do funny things in the moment like strike a Yoga pose or pull a funny face with her mouth or roll up her lips so you could see her teeth. This kind of spontaneous, 'in the moment' stuff made me laugh and helped immensely when I experienced feelings of profound sadness.

Demi took me on this amazing walk. It's called the Tolkien trail in the Ribble Valley. J.R.R Tolkien wrote 'The Lord of the Rings' whilst he was teaching at Stonyhurst College in the Ribble Valley, and many people believe that 'Middle Earth' is based on this area. It does feel like the film and it has breathtaking views of nature. As we walked we laughed and I told her about my experiences seeing Karen and Ashleigh. She said she knew of Ashleigh but then, as we continued to walk, a feeling of profound sadness started to overwhelm me. I began to withdraw into myself and feel very sad. It was as if a dark cloud could come over me at any time and there was no real explanation for it.

We continued with the walk and Demi, sensing this, was great. She just left me to be in my space. At times I felt bad but there was nothing I could do to change it. It was as if someone had poured concrete down my throat or stitched my lips together. I just couldn't speak. I was consumed by a kind of numbness. There were no words to describe it - all I knew was that it was definitely nothing to do with Demi and everything to do with my grief.

We finished the walk and Demi explained that she understood how I was feeling and that if I wanted my own space it was fine. I said to her that if she was ok I wanted a few days to myself to sit with what was going on inside of me.

When I got back to my apartment my phone pinged. It was Demi and the message read 'John I forgot to tell you, there is a series on Netflix by Ricky Gervais. It is really good and I know you'll like it. I reckon it will be very helpful with what you are currently going through.'

Although I do not watch a lot of TV, I thought, 'What have I got to lose?' So I found the programme Demi had referred to. It was called After Life and it was the storyline of Tony Johnson whose wife dies of cancer. My God, I was in floods of tears but I couldn't stop watching it. Everything that this character was going through with his grief was describing exactly what was going on in me and it was very funny, too. I had never really watched many of Ricky Gervais' programmes but this man was a very talented man and he had come to me at a time when I was going through the worst point in my life. For the next couple of days I drank beer, ate whatever I wanted to (crisps and cake, and other not so good stuff!) watched Netflix, slept, turned off my phone and shut out the world. I told myself that I was entitled to have a blowout. My Mum had died. I told myself that I would share all this with Karen in our next meeting.

The rest of the week followed the same pattern. And then Friday came. I don't know if it was the After Life programme or the blowout but I started my day saying to myself, 'Right John, let's get this book written for your Mum and do our best to get back into the swing of things.'

I went to my appointment with Karen and I told her about the Ricky Gervais programme on Netflix which she said she'd heard of. I explained, "Karen you need to tell as many people as you can. It's amazing for anybody that has lost a loved one. "

I then opened up and was honest with Karen. I told her about the drinking behind closed doors, that I had done this when Kathleen and my dad had died but that I had an awareness around it and that, if I felt like it was getting out of control, I would talk to someone. That is why I wanted to tell Karen.

Karen explained that it was common to drink alcohol. Lots of people drink when they have lost someone they love, but she wanted me to know that alcohol was a depressant and reminded me that I needed to be aware of how I was emotionally.

I shared with Karen my feelings of depression and not wanting to be around anybody. I also told her that starting to write the book had given me focus, knowing that a lot of good could come out of this terrible situation. Karen asked me if I had read a book called Grief Works by Julia Samuel. I said I had loads of books on the go so she suggested I get it on Audible.

Before I knew it, our session was over and it was time to see Ashleigh. I was really ready for some Reiki. Ashleigh came and collected me from the reception area and with her lovely calm presence said, "So how are you doing, John?" I explained that I'd been up and down. We began talking about what had been going on since we last met and I opened up about the drinking and the depression. Then, to my surprise, she said, "Do you watch Netflix? There is this series called After Life. I couldn't believe it. What were the chances of that? I explained to her that Demi had mentioned it and a few other friends since and that I was watching it and it was helping me massively with my grief.

I asked Ashleigh, "Could I have some more Reiki please, as it really helped last time?"

She replied, "If that's what you feel like you need then we will give you some good reiki healing," and the same thing happened again. I was out like a light!

This time I saw lots of amazing colours, especially indigo, and, before I knew it, I could hear Ashleigh saying, "There you go, John. When you are ready, there is a glass of water." When

I came around I told Ashleigh how, in the short amount of time coming to see her and Karen, their kindness had helped me massively. It was bringing me through my grief and helping me start to get my life back on track. Their help was making me think about doing things for my self-care and taking good care of myself. Ashleigh then gave me a genuine and caring smile and said, "Same time next week, John?"

I said, "You better believe it. I can't wait!"

Grief Works

***

That week I started to reflect on everything that had been going on inside of me, emotionally and mentally. All the experiences I was having made me think about where I might be on the bereavement curve. Even though everyone experiences these stages differently, I felt that I was slowly getting through the grief stage.

I knew that practising my affirmations was helping me massively, especially when I found myself self-sabotaging. I then heard Karen's lovely voice in my head saying, 'Grief Works'. I knew what I had to do – buy the book on Audible and listen to it at home and in the car.

I downloaded it with the Audible app and WOW! From the minute I started listening to the book, it was so comforting to hear Julia describe her experience as a grief counsellor. She shares case studies of the many clients that she has counselled over the years. It was like she was in my head when she described what grief felt like.

She started the book with a case study of someone who had lost a loving partner, and all the case studies I listened to gave me hope and strength. More importantly, listening to the book brought about something magical in me. It inspired me to get my head down and to start to put the book together. I wanted Taking Her to the Door to help others who were feeling the pain that I and countless human beings had to go through when faced with the heartbreaking reality of losing someone they love.

I got back to my apartment and I began to look at all the notes I had made in my times of emotional despair. The grief began to come together like a jigsaw puzzle. All the pieces slotted into place: Richard coming to see Mum and his book with the numbers, making the notes for taking her to the door, the meltdowns, wanting to be alone, talking with Sarah, meeting Demi, the counselling and Reiki, The After Life series, The Julia Samuel book "Grief Works".

The final piece was when Mum had said to me that the next book I'd write would be better than the last one. What were the chances of all this happening? It was meant to be. I was supposed to go through all this pain so I could write this book to give hope and strength to others who were going through cancer.

I had inspired myself. I could see just how the book was hopefully going to make a massive difference in people's lives. I took a break, went and made a cup of tea and then received a random message out of the blue. It was from my good friend Anna Lisa from Victoria Island in Canada. It read: 'Hi John. I have been travelling around the Outer Hebrides and I've heard about your Mum. If it's ok with you I want to come and see you before I go back to Canada. I can change my flight time and I will come and see you. Here is my number.'

This was amazing. I loved Anna Lisa. We'd met many years ago at a global meeting in Aberdeen and we both were specially selected to represent our countries, working with other people from around the world to see what positive ideas we could generate to put something back into society.

Anna Lisa and I got on like a house on fire and had always kept in touch. She is an excellent photographer, teacher and, like me, loves to travel and enjoy nature. I knew she would be up for going on a good walk but where could I take her?

Where I live there are so many great walks. I phoned Anna Lisa and she answered the phone "John, I am so sorry to hear about your Mum. I've been travelling and I want to come and see you. I can get a train tomorrow."

The following day I met Anna Lisa at Blackburn train station.

She is always laughing. The minute she came off the train we hugged and laughed. When she laughs she makes a snorting noise like a pig. It really does make me laugh. I explained to her that I had something lovely planned and with the limited time we had together I wanted to take her on one of my favourite local walks.

We dropped off her luggage at my place and then I took her to Tockholes Woods. Tockholes has a beautiful lake. I showed Anna Lisa a bench that I sit on overlooking the lake. That bench had given me the inspiration for my Kindness Matters book.

She was blown away by the stunning scenery. The view from the bench is of the reservoir which looked still and deep. The smooth water reflected the clear blue sky and the fir and pine trees that lined it. The place was silent apart from the sound of birdsong. As we continued to walk she stopped to take photos at every new scene. We walked through the forest, which is about a good 4-mile hike and as we walked I began to tell her everything I had been going through. I told her the story about hearing the voice to write the book and all the coincidences.

She said, "John, there are no coincidences. There is just a lot we do not know. I've lost good friends and have had some bizarre experiences that cannot be rationally explained. There is more to this life than what we think we know."

It was just what I needed to hear. I told her that Karen the counsellor had recommended I listen to Grief Works, and Demi and Ashleigh directed me towards the Afterlife programme. These and all the other connections brought it all to life for my Mum's book.

We made our way out of the woods and I took Anna Lisa to a lovely country pub in Abbey Village called The Hare and Hounds. We sat there and laughed and talked about some of our experiences working in education. Anna Lisa worked in the same field as me, working with kids from deprived and challenging backgrounds. We were putting the world to rights over a good pint of ale. She loves England and she loves our old fashioned English pubs. We sat in the back of the pub, near the old coal fire, and we talked about Mum.

"John, this book that you're writing, it's amazing. Only someone like you could do this, when you are going through all this pain, putting something together for others having the same experience," said Anna Lisa.

I explained to her that journaling, meditation, affirmations and seeing Karen and Ashleigh had all helped massively but the one big thing that had done it for me was talking to friends and family, Sarah and Demi and letting them see how vulnerable I was.

Many people suffer in silence, whether it's with grief or mental health. I wanted mine and Mum's story and experiences to help stop that and help others with their transition. I shared with Anna Lisa how grateful I was to the hospice for giving me the free counselling sessions and the alternative therapy. We talked about how Reiki had helped me so much. I was going to speak with the hospice the following day to see about putting a date in the diary for me to have the book finished; then do a fundraiser for the book launch.

I said, "Come on, we'd better get home and get you some rest. You have a flight to catch tomorrow."

In Loving Memory

***

The following morning I made Anna Lisa breakfast and then we made our way to the train station. We hugged and cried and I promised her that I would come and visit her beautiful country and speak in some of her schools. She said, "Listen John, your Mum will always be with you and the book is going to help so many people. Keep in touch and let me know if you need anything."

I gave her a smile and said, "You bet ya."

I made my way to my last session at the hospice and even though the grief came and went, I was doing my best to focus on everything I had to be grateful for. I made my way to the reception and they kindly asked me to wait in the seating area. As usual, I came with an awareness of all the people who would be in the hospice preparing to make their way to the door and all the families who had to pick up the pieces afterwards. Then I started to think that when I finish the book how much it could help balance their grief and help with their transition.

As I was having all these thoughts I heard a voice say, "John? John is that you? John Magee?"

I replied saying, "Yes that's me."

The woman said, "My name is Catherine. I know all about you. I have read your book Kindness Matters and Karen the counsellor has told me that you have started writing a book that you want to donate to the hospice." Catherine was the head of fundraising at the hospice and is very passionate about raising money to support it.

It felt like it was happening again, all these connections. I said to Catherine, "I want to do more than that. I want to do a book signing as a fundraiser. I am pretty well known and I have quite a big following on social media as The Kindness Coach."

Catherine explained that due to them being a charity everything is very highly regulated and that all charitable donations and fundraisers had to go through management. She could arrange a meeting to meet with the bosses that she knew would be delighted with my kind proposal. Catherine said, "When would you like to have a meeting?"

"How about after my treatment? Let's strike while the iron's hot!"

She was delighted and said, "That's fantastic. I'll see you later."

On walking into Karen's room and knowing this was our last session, I had mixed emotions. I had got very close and fond of Karen. She was a beautiful kind soul and was very good at helping others with their grief. In her strong Lancashire accent, she asked, "So how are you doing?"

I explained that, since seeing her and Ashleigh, a lot of positives had come about in my life. I told her that I'd just bumped into Catherine and the plans for doing a fundraiser with the book about my Mum's death.

She said, "That is fantastic!"

I said, "You don't get it though, Karen. When you recommended that book Grief Works, it was like a massive domino that kick-started a chain reaction of events. It was as if it brought all the pieces together of what had been happening in my life and I could finally see a way of getting through the transition with my grief." She was delighted.

I said to Karen, "Anyway, to thank you for all your kindness, I've brought you a signed copy of my book Kindness Matters and that's not the last of it. How would you like it if I write about you in Taking Her to the Door? She laughed and said, "Stop it – you're making me blush!"

I joked with her and said, "You'll be famous! People will be asking for your autograph!" On a serious note, I told her how indebted I was to her and that, when I do the launch, I would like her to come as a guest. She agreed. We hugged, shed a tear or two, and she wished me all the best with my future.

I waited in the seating area again and then there she was the angel, the softly spoken, amazing healer Ashleigh. "Hi, John. It's good to see you," she said in her soft calming voice, "So how are you?"

I said to Ashleigh the same as what I'd said to Karen about how coming to see her is something I would not have done but it was the best decision of my life. I told her how grateful I was for her kindness and I thanked her for all she had done for me - the After Life programme and the introduction to Reiki. As I said that she replied, "I have a gift for you. I have contacted my Reiki teacher, Maureen, and she said she is going to contact you so that if you want to help others with it then you can." I was absolutely thrilled.

I then had the deepest Reiki session ever and once again with lots of beautiful colours. I woke to, "John there is a glass of water. Get up when you are ready," and yes, 30 minutes had flown by.

I also gave a copy of Kindness Matters to Ashleigh and asked if I could mention her in my mum's book and if she would come to the book signing as that was what I was going to do for the hospice, as a thank you. She said she would be honoured.

I shared with her that I was going to see Catherine straight after this meeting with a view to discussing the book and how I wanted it to be in my Mum's late memory, and to raise money to pay for counselling or holistic therapy or anything the hospice needed to raise funds for. I gave Ashleigh one last hug and just as she always did she gave me that angelic silent smile, nodded her head and said, "Take care, John."

Once I'd left the therapy room I made my way to have the meeting with Catherine for the fundraiser. I began to get a warm feeling inside, that I was on the cusp of something magical. These past months have been a roller coaster of emotions and they still were at times. I sat down with Catherine and shared with her my vision.

I explained that I did not want a penny of the proceeds and that I would gladly give my time freely and invite 100+ guests who would all pay £20 a ticket and get a free signed copy of the book. I also said that I would bring some influential guests/celebrity friends to generate real interest.

And then after the event, every copy of the book that would be sold on Amazon or in the hospice would go to the charity.

Catherine could not believe what I was saying. Catherine said, "You do know that this is going to help a lot of people, John!"

I explained that if it only helped one person receive the care and compassion that I had received off Karen and Ashleigh, and all volunteers and hospice staff, then that would be enough for me.

At this point I did not know a date when the book would be ready. All I knew was that I had to trust the process over the coming months, and that, along with my motivational speaking and my work in building my global Kindness Matters movement, I would somehow find the time to have the book finished and be honoured to donate it to the hospice.

Catherine said, "Well, on that note, we will look forward to you contacting us in the foreseeable future!"

I made my way to the car and I sat in the car thinking to myself that this was like a dream within a dream. When would be a good time to release the book? What about October, my Mum's anniversary? As I thought about it, the phone rang. It was my good friend Debbie Wright. What were the chances of that? Debbie was the one who had taken her Mum to the door and inspired me to share that story with my Mum.

I said, "Debs, you are not going to believe where I am? I'm outside the hospice and I've just finished all my therapy and had a meeting with the fundraising team. I've shared with them what I want to do in my Mum's memory and how I am going to donate all the proceeds from the book to the hospice."

Debbie said, "That is lovely. When are you thinking of doing it?"

I explained that I would have loved to have done it on October the 24th but as I was working on making November the official months for schools to take the 'Kindness Matters 30-day Challenge' I didn't want it to get lost as I would be in the paper and on the radio for 'Kindness Matters.'

Debbie said, "I have a suggestion John and I will only tell you if you promise me that you can let me and Brian come to the fundraiser."

I laughed and said, "You are funny! Go on, what are you thinking?"

She said, "Well, I know how hard it still is for me now, as a mother who misses her mother, so why not March 22, 2020? Do you know what date that is?"

I shook my head. "It's Mother's day." I was speechless.

That was it! That was the cherry on the cake. I said, "Mrs Wright, I love you. That is it. That is the date we will release the book."

That will be the day, in loving memory of my Mum, Pat Magee, aka Nana Pat.

Epilogue

***

I hope you enjoyed *Taking Her to the Door* and it gave you, a friend, or a family member comfort.   More importantly, I hope it gave you hope and strength. It has been exactly a year since my Mum died and made her transition. Because I work in education I had dedicated the October half term to get the book finished on the anniversary of my Mum's passing 24th October. I have to confess the one thing I did not realise was how going back over the chapters would bring up so much more of the grief but what this has helped me understand is there is so much growth in grief.

Over the last twelve months, it has been a roller coaster of emotion and it still is. I believe losing someone we love is the most difficult experience we have to go through in life. I have learnt so much about grief and I am still learning and growing. I hope that what I have shared in the book will help you balance your grief and give you some of the resources that helped me.

As I sit here now writing this, I am reflecting on all the events that happened from the minute I was given the news that my Mum was going to die from cancer. I am also recollecting all the things that brought this book to life, which I now describe as 'connecting the dots':

- The meeting with Debbie Wright after the news and being in shock and her sharing the story she used for her Mother's transition, 'Taking her to the door'
- Hearing the voice after speaking with Ray outside my Mum's flat (to write a book)
- My Mum said to me the next book I write will be better than the last one I wrote
- Richard McCann's book, Just a Man, giving Mum strength about the afterlife and the number 44
- The number 44 and Mum dying at 22:44 2+2=4, 44 hospice 4 days 4 nights
- Meeting Demi and her being a Reiki healer and inspiring me to watch After Life
- Meeting Karen the counsellor and her suggesting Julia Samuel's book Grief Works
- Meeting Ashleigh who inspired me to watch After Life and being introduced to Maureen, her Reiki teacher, who is now my teacher

- Meeting Catherine at the hospice and her team putting together the fundraiser for the book signing and annual fundraiser
- Debbie Wright, March 22nd Mother's Day, the book release 2020

Were all of these just coincidences? I will not have anybody tell me that all these events are coincidences. What I am about to tell you, you can take with a pinch of salt or you can accept it.

The week after Anna Lisa went back to Canada, I went back into the Hare and Hounds pub after a lovely walk to clear my head. I sat down in the same place where we'd sat the previous week. I looked out of the window and began thinking about Mum. I started to say to myself silently how grateful I was for her and that I knew I had done my best to give her a good send off and that I'd taken the best care of her that I could. Mum and I had always joked about death and one time I'd said to her that I didn't want her to blow the lights in the house, as that's what had happened when Kathleen and Dad died. Coincidence? Mum had laughed and joked but she said she would never do anything to frighten me.

I went to the toilet in the pub and came back. As I sat down, on the window sill there was a glass jar, the ones that have solar power, and it began to flash. I asked the young girl who was cleaning the cutlery, if she had turned it on and she said to me that they come on automatically when it is dark.

I was mesmerized. It was still daylight outside. I was just about to say to her that it's not yet dark when something said to me 'it's Mum'. I looked at my watch and it was 4:44pm. I could not believe it. I got on my phone and videoed the whole experience and sent it to Richard McCann on WhatsApp. Richard promptly replied and said, "Yep that's your Mum alright."

In my heart of hearts, I believe that this was my Mum. Since Mum passed away I've visited my dad's grave and noticed his plot number is 44. Also, my Mum died at 22:44pm, 2+2=4, 44. Mum was in the hospice for 4 days and 4 nights. I really don't know what all these 4s are for but if you look up Doreen Virtue, the number 44 means "The Angels are giving you extra comfort, love and support right now. Ask them for help with everything, and listen to their guidance and through your intuition."

Whether it is true or not, it has given me comfort and support and I take that number as a sign from Mum that I am on track with things in my life. I will stop it now with the mumbo gumbo and get back on track. There are many positives that will come from your grief and it will take time.

Everybody's grief experience is different from that of others, and I believe that it is a transition, and you will get through it.

Out of all of this experience, even though Mum was only in the hospice for 4 days and 4 nights, the way she was treated, with respect and dignity, was incredible. The hospice is not a place to be fearful of - Mum had her own private room, with shower room, TV, chairs and beds not to mention the incredible aftercare I received.

Whether you have been through the experience of a hospice or not, I would like to encourage you, the reader, to do what a lot of people do. That is, to donate clothes, household items or maybe even leave something to a hospice in your will. For me, while I am still breathing, I am going to donate something that money can't buy, and that is my time. The work and time that the volunteers and fundraisers give to help others is incredible. Your currency is your time - just imagine if you only give one hour a week, what that could do.

On a final note can I kindly ask you, the reader, to recommend this book to anybody you know who is going through cancer or has been through cancer. Also, if you would take the time to review the book on Amazon, this will help raise more funds for the Hospice, as all royalty payments will be going to the charity.

Thank you for your kindness.

John Magee

Resources

***

The Bereavement Curve

***

I have written this section of the book in the hope that it helps you to see where you might be in your own grief and provide you with some insight into where you are on your grief journey. The model I have shared is one that most bereavement counsellors are familiar with. The model is not set in stone as each of us experiences grief in our own way. However, there are common stages and this example may allow you to hopefully see where you are.

I also wanted to share with you the power of affirmations. I became interested in the power of affirmation many years ago from the amazing work of the late great Louise Hay, 'The Queen of Affirmations'. Affirmations really do help, particularly when you are aware that you are overthinking things and find yourself saying unhelpful self-talk - you know, that little voice in your head that likes to give you a hard time.

A positive affirmation can shut it down.

If you find yourself like that or not, take a look at the bereavement curve and ask yourself where you are in your life right now in terms of the bereavement process. Then read the section and practise the affirmations as often as possible. I found it useful to have them in my notes on my smartphone and then, once I'd mastered one, I would move on to the next one. Each day I would repeatedly say them silently to myself, or when I got home I would go to the mirror, look at myself and say them out loud to myself.

If you are willing to work outside of your comfort zone and practise affirmations daily, I assure you that this practice will do you more good than harm.

CHANGE - A TIME OF LOSS, GAIN AND NEW OPPORTUNITY

"Life is good -
now I can live with my loss"

LIFE WITH NEW
INSIGHT AND
UNDERSTANDING

"It can't be true"

"Here I come..!"   NEW LEARNING
AND HOPE

DENIAL

SHOCK   "Oh no"

"Here we go again"   RE-CONNECTING
WITHOUT LEARNING

ANGER   "It's their fault"

SELF-DOUBT   "Maybe if I had.."

"Now what..?"   ACCEPTANCE/LETTING GO

PINING/SEARCHING   "It's all my fault"

"What if I.."   EMERGENCE

GUILT

SADNESS

"What's the point"

DEPRESSION/DESPAIR

Denial

***

Denial is the first stage which we have to face when someone we love is told that they have cancer. I suppose it comes from not wanting to accept that something so dreadful is happening. It is easier to think that it has been a mistake, a wrong diagnosis or something not so bad. This is particularly true when the diagnosis is a terminal one. It simply can't be happening.

It is naturally very hard to accept and believe that the person you love is going to die. Death may be the only inevitable fact in our lives but it is not something we want to stare in the face. You try not to panic but there is an overwhelming feeling that this must be some kind of bad dream and one that you hope you will wake up from soon.

In my case, it wasn't just me who was in denial. My mum had the growth in her neck for some time but didn't want to get it diagnosed, denying to herself what it was.

Despite our feelings, some of you reading this will be in

the position that you have to be strong and resilient for other members of your family. For me, I had to keep telling myself that I had to be as strong as I could for my Mum and her grandkids (my children).

It is hard; and at times it feels impossible. But you are no different from me. You will cope. Don't get me wrong - you'll have good days and bad days but you have more strength than you could ever possibly know. What you have to do is to take one step at a time and one day at a time. Do your best to tell yourself that you have the resilience and that this will get you through this challenging time.

What I found helped was speaking to other people. For me, it was an aunt and one of my best friends, Scott. This helped tremendously. Talk to someone you have a good relationship with. However, it may be that your closest confidant is also affected or that you don't feel that you can speak so openly to friends. In that case, go and see your doctor and express how you are feeling. Sadly, your doctor will have had many, many conversations like this. The worst thing you can do is bottle up your emotions and not speak to anyone. Not talking will do you and your family no good.

It is perfectly normal to be in denial and, until you speak with the professionals and find out how this process works, you may feel that your feelings are unnatural or that you are the only person who feels like this. Remember, there are various stages which we have to go through. At each stage, it will help if you find a sense of balance and identify where you currently are on your journey. It will also help you recognise your progress through your own transition.

Points to consider

- Do your best to not let your mind race ahead of itself or overthink
- There are many benefits to be had in speaking with friends and family
- Speak with a professional, e.g. doctor, counsellor, life coach
- Reassure your loved ones that you're in it together
- Remind yourself that you can get through this.

Helpful Affirmations

Peace is the result of training my mind to process life as it is rather than how I think it could be.

I bring myself into the present moment and process life as it is.

I am open and willing to accept the reality of the situation.

It is safe for me to clearly see what is happening.

I open my eyes and accept the situation.

Whenever you find your mind running away with itself, repeat an affirmation(s) as often as possible.

Shock

***

For some of you, the feeling of shock may have occurred before the feeling of denial. For others, it occurs after, or even at, the same time. Initially, you have refused to accept that the person you love is dying or has a terminal diagnosis. At some point, however, you have to accept it but, with the acceptance that it really is happening, comes a sense of shock. This stage is often talked about in bereavement counselling.

Nothing prepares you for it. Even if, at the back of your mind, you have been thinking it may be happening, when you hear the actual word 'cancer', it truly is a shock to the system. Knowing that the person you love so dearly has the disease and that it's terminal, makes you feel numb and disconnected, often unable to function. For most of us, this feeling of shock is short-lived, although others will experience this for much longer. You just have to remember that it is natural to feel this way and that eventually this feeling will pass.

The thing is, once you have dealt with the shock and denial, you begin to think about what you can do to help. Believe me, there is so much you can do and the first thing to do is be open and talk. Talk to your friends and family but also talk to the person with the diagnosis. Whatever you are feeling, their feelings will be as powerful, if not more powerful.

Start talking. Take one step at a time and do your best to keep your composure and reassure everyone that, whatever happens, you are in it together. There may not be the happy ending you want but you will get through it.

Don't get me wrong, it won't be a walk in the park and at times it will feel like hell on earth, but by communicating with your family and the people who are close to you this will help you deal with your feelings. You will begin to somehow gain acceptance. It's all about taking small steps, taking one small step at a time.

Points to consider

- Reassure everyone including yourself that you will get through this
- Affirm to yourself you can get through this
- Practise, practise, practise the affirmations as often as possible

Helpful Affirmations

I am strong, resilient and I will get through this is my own time. I love and approve of myself.

I accept this moment and I am open to all the possibilities with this new challenge in my life.

Remember, whenever you find your mind running away with itself, repeat one or more of the affirmations as often as possible.

Anger, Guilt and Sadness

***

Looking back now I see how when things got overwhelming for me, my Mum and all the family.

We were angry. My Mum was angry - she raged about the fact that she was dying. She felt cheated out of her future. She was right to be angry. What felt difficult at the time was how she sometimes took that anger out on me. That, too, is inevitable, as you are more open and honest with those closest to you.

I experienced anger too. I had already lost my dad and my sister, and that small family unit of the four of us would soon become just me. I too felt that I was being cheated and was angry for myself but also angry for my children, that they would lose their Nan Pat.

I also battled with that feeling that I had to be strong for everyone, including my Mum. When I felt weak and unable to cope, I felt angry with myself.

At times I got angry with my Mum. We had a number of big arguments before she died, in which we both said things we immediately regretted. I know now that these arguments were born out of the anger we were both experiencing. This inevitably resulted in feelings of guilt. What kind of person argues with a dying woman? The truth is - an angry one.

Allow yourself and your loved ones to be angry. It is a natural reaction. It will pass.

I also felt a tremendous sense of guilt. When my Mum was dying, it was the guilt that I had not been, or was now not being, a good enough son. I wanted so desperately to make my Mum proud but the actual process of caring for her was so difficult at times that when I couldn't cope, I felt immense guilt that I was letting her down and that I had not done enough. The reassurance I received from the nursing team helped tremendously though.

I also experienced great guilt after Mum's death. I felt guilty when I did anything that brought me happiness or pleasure. I think I felt most guilt about my relationship with Demi. How could I be enjoying life and moving on so quickly after my Mum's death? The consequence was this feeling of guilt.

We also experienced overwhelming sadness, times when we sobbed in toilets, wept together, cried alone. The guilt can turn into sadness or anger at yourself.

In reality, these emotions are all mixed up together, different ones surfacing at different times, triggered by what can seem insignificant things. Throughout it all though, you often have that inner voice, giving you a hard time, saying that you should have done this or should not have done that. You can become your own worst enemy.

If you find yourself using the word should, can I encourage you to change the word to could, as this latter word gives you options and choices to change things. 'Should', on the other hand, always implies that you have done something wrong and it's too late to change it.

You need to remember this is what cancer does to people. It emotionally and mentally challenges you as you have never been challenged before. What is important is to remember that, whatever you say or do in those moments of sheer frustration and anger, you are doing your best until you find a better way of handling the situation.

Points to consider

- You are always doing your best until you find a better way to handle the situation
- If you find yourself saying the word 'should' change it to the word 'could'

- Love and accept yourself - you are doing your best
- If and when you feel angry, guilty or sad, be open about it and talk about how feel.

Helpful Affirmations

I allow all unhelpful thoughts and feelings to dissolve.

I slow down my thoughts and breathe easily.

I open up to thinking kinder thoughts.

I choose to look at the situation from a kinder and healthier perspective.

Remember, whenever you find your mind running away with itself, repeat one or more of the affirmations as often as possible.

Depression

***

I had read and was familiar with the stages in the Bereavement Curve but, to be honest, depression crept up on me. I knew about depression and, like most of us, I have known family and friends who have had depression but it wasn't something that I thought I would have myself.

I had been experiencing the inevitable sadness that comes with the death of a loved one. Then one day I realised that what I was experiencing was more than just a deep sadness, but depression itself. It knocked me sideways. As you'll remember in the book I started to drink more alcohol, I wanted to be alone and I didn't want to talk to anyone - all of these were symptoms of depression.

You may feel the need to be alone. Sometimes we need that time to heal and be reflective. Sometimes the need for solitude arises from the view that we would not be good company and would spoil things for other people. Sometimes the thought of being with others fills you with a sense of anxiety or distress.

However, you do need to recognise the difference between feeling sad or melancholic and being depressed.

I knew that hiding myself away from others was doing me no good. It's fine to take time to adjust but when you reach the point when those feelings start to consume you, you need to recognise it for what it is. If you can, revisit the chapter on depression (page 137) and if you feel like I was feeling or not, accept the need for solitude but let people know how you are feeling. Like in the previous pages on the bereavement curve, the key is to begin to talk and open up with a friend, family member or counsellor. Talking really does help to express those deep, painful thoughts and feelings. The thing is, our thoughts can get the better of us and then we can end up in a downward spiral. That is why, when you find yourself in this position, do your best to say the affirmation I have given as an example.

For some of us, the feeling of depression is relatively short-lived. For others, it is not. Please be aware of your own mental health and the mental health of those around you. Don't assume that just because someone presents as being fine on the outside that they are fine on the inside. At times we become so wrapped up in our own issues that we do not see what is going on around us. Talk to each other.

Points to consider

- Be mindful of your thoughts and feelings
- Look up help for depression on Google or Youtube. There are lots of amazing resources out there to help with your transition
- Remind yourself that it is perfectly normal to feel this way
- Practising affirmations will only do more good than harm
- If you feel it is getting too much, reach out and talk to someone

Helpful Affirmations

- I am open and willing to ask for help.
- I hold my own hand and take one day at a time.
- I focus my attention on supporting myself.
- I care for myself like I would a good friend.

Remember, whenever you find your mind running away with itself, repeat one or more of the affirmations as often as possible.

Letting Go and Acceptance

***

How long does it take for one to let go and accept that the person we love has gone and that we have to move forward with our lives? How long is a piece of string?

For each one of us, the journey through grief is our very own personal experience. The path taken and the steps trodden are our own. All I know now, as I look back, is that there was a black cloud following me and then one day I woke up and the cloud was not quite so dark. As the days passed the cloud finally lifted and I could see blue skies again. I don't recall how and when this happened to me but I do remember looking at myself and saying, 'Right John, you did your best and your Mum would not want you to hold on to this sad feeling anymore. She would want you to move forward and accept that life is what it is.'

One of the best ways I dealt with this was to envisage the time when it's my turn to pass through the door. I know I would not want to see my kids and family consumed by their grief for me. I would want them to move forward with their lives and let go. I knew that my Mum would want this for me.

It does take time to adjust. You will get there. Keep yourself busy. Talk to the people you love when they are around. Tell them all the exciting things you are working on and doing with your life. Even start a new hobby or, if you are up for it, maybe become part of a support group and help others with their grief.

There will be a massive hole in your life. The first celebration or birthday or anniversary will be incredibly difficult. A piece of music will break your heart. You will want to pick the phone up to call them, then remember. You will miss them more than you thought possible but your life will continue and you will be happy again.

Points to consider

- Talk about happy memories and how you are beginning to move forward with your life to friends and family and work colleagues
- Consider joining a support group or volunteering and doing something that has value to you
- Consider doing a new hobby or even learning an instrument
- Remind yourself daily that you are making progress

Helpful Affirmations

- I release all negative thoughts and feelings.
- It is safe for me to feel good.
- I accept what is and move forward with ease.
- I am open to embracing life fully.

Remember, whenever you find your mind running away with itself, repeat one or more of the affirmations as often as possible.

Life with New Understanding and New Hope

***

It's been over 12 months since Mum made her transition. During those 12 months, there has been so much change and growth. There is an old saying, that there is nothing more certain in life than change. Ain't that just the truth!

Probably the most important thing I have learnt during this time is how very precious life is. Never take it for granted. Appreciate your family and friends. Life is short and we do not know what the future will hold. Appreciate the beauty of our world - see the rainbows in puddles, see the beauty in all of it. Talk to people whenever you can. Be kind because you never know what is going on in someone else's life. Live life - it is the only one we have.

Wherever you are in your journey through grief know it will take time to adjust. It does for every single human being. Nothing prepares you for it but it is something that we all have to go through. Believe me, there is a light at the end of the tunnel.

In your own time, you will develop a new understanding of the loss of your loved one. You will learn so much about yourself. You will learn how to come to terms with your loss and how to live with it.

I am eternally grateful for my life and I accept that my life has meaning and that what I do makes a difference. At one point I felt hopeless and powerless and I accept that now. I also accept that is sometimes a part of life.

I would do anything to hear Mum's voice one more time or for her to give me a good telling off! The fact of the matter is that it is not going to happen; and I now accept that.

I give thanks daily and tell myself how grateful I am to have had her for all my life, that she lived to be 75 years old. I know not everyone gets that and that whatever time we get we need to be grateful for it all. My grief has brought so much good into my life and made me appreciate life for what it is - natural beauty, the beauty of life. What a precious thing!

I wish you all the best for the rest of your journeys and I hope that you, like me, will come to learn all the beauty and hope this life has to offer.

Points to consider

- Look back on the period of time of your grief and see the progress you have made

- Accept that there is nothing more certain than change
- Look for all the good in your life now that has come out of your loss
- Be grateful for life and all that it teaches you
- Celebrate the beauty in life in everything you do
- Practise gratitude daily
- Believe in the positive power of practising your affirmations daily

Helpful Affirmations

- I embrace every day with an open mind and a grateful heart.
- I have so much to be grateful for.
- I treasure every precious moment and live life to the full.
- I fully participate in life.
- I am free to move forward with love in my heart.
- Life is good!
- I support myself with kind and encouraging thoughts.
- I trust the flow of life to provide new understanding.
- I am guided and supported every step of the way.

Remember, whenever you find your mind running away with itself, repeat one or more of the affirmations as often as possible.

Other useful information

***

There are plenty of great books and resources out there and many are also available on Audible. Here are a few that helped me along the journey and that I would recommend:

Books

Kindness Matters - John Magee

Just a Man - Richard McCann

Grief Works - Julia Samuels

The Power Of Now - Eckart Tolle

You Can Heal Your Life - Louise Hay

Mindfulness Made Simple - Olly Doyle

I also found the following on Netflix which helped me put things into perspective. Hopefully, they will do the same for you.

Netflix

Be Here Now -The Andy Whitfield Story

AfterLife - Ricky Gervais

The Call To Courage - Brené Brown

We are always safe
It is only change
From the moment we are born
We are preparing to be embraced by the Light once more
Position yourself for maximum peace
Angels surround you
They are guiding you each step of the way
However you choose your exit
It will be perfect for you
Everything will happen in the perfect time-sequence
This is a time for joy and rejoicing
You are on your way home
As we all are.
Louise Hay

Special thanks to my Auntie Moo aka Auntie Olive for being the best aunt a nephew could ever wish for. All my love now and always, your favourite nephew George :-)

My fantastic cousin Lee who has been the brother I have always wished for. For being there for me when my grief brought me to my knees and his beautiful wife, our Sarah, Holly, Evan and Grace.

Leona, Millie and Lucas for being the best kids/grandkids ever and making my Mum so proud.

To all my beautiful family for their unconditional love - Auntie Roz Bo, Bo and family for your support to me and my Mum.

Catherine, Benjamin, Michelle, Sam and family, Olive and family, Marie and family, David & Lesley Gaffing and family, Sarah Wright and family, Denise and Bernadette, Patrick, Claire & Family.

My cousin Sarah Magee, William, Katlyn, the twins, Leah and Mariah, for always being there for me in those times of need.

Elaine and all the district nursing team for all your kindness and everything you did for my Mum. She loved you, Elaine, more than you will ever know - no doubt you will get that in the book.

Pat, George, Tracy, Pete & Conrad, Barbara for being such good friends to my Mum.

Darren and all the staff at Oswaldtwistle Funeral Directors. You are a very good friend Darren. Thank you for all your support and most of all your friendship.

Father McCarthy and Father Paul and all Saint Anne's Church for all the love and compassion for Mum.

Father Barry for taking good care of me and being a friend and telling it as it was and for everything you have always done for me and my family - 'The worst-dressed man in town is the tailor'!

All the staff at Old Mother Redcap for all the happy memories you gave my Mum and all our family at the wake.

Scott and Victoria Moon for helping me balance my grief in those many times of need.

Thanks to Debbie Wright and Brian for all your kindness and bringing the title 'Taking Her to the Door' to my attention; you are a good friend, and I am grateful for all the coffees and great food.

Paul Bridge and Peps for all your support as a friend and brother. POI

Chris and Glenda Grimsley from NLP in The North West for your kindness and endless coaching. You are both good friends.

Anna Lisa, my beautiful Canadian friend, who has the best piggy laugh ever. I would never have guessed from our meeting in 2012 at The Gordon Cook Conversations that we would become such good friends. I will never forget your kindness and how you took the time to come and see me after Mum's transition - a very special lady you are.

Arthur Luke. I am indebted to you for everything that you have done for me since the day we met. It is priceless. As always, you always deliver. What you have done for 'Taking Her to the Door' is just how I envisioned it, and my Mum would be a very proud Mother seeing this. #Tigger

Jo Watson aka Ghosty for always being there for me and picking up my grammar and punctuation and being such a good friend.

Nathan Damour aka "Natdog" for always being there and all the fantastic curries and laughs at the hardest of times. Love you, Bro!

Big DG, thank you, Dave, for all the things you told me to say to my Mum before she made her transition and for all your support with the funeral and aftermath your good friend Curly JC #Creamofthecroft

The Hospice - Ashleigh, Karen the counsellor, Sophie, Jen, Cat and the amazing staff that make such a positive difference in people's lives.

Kareplus - Kirstie, Donna, Samfa, Jess and all the staff for making my Mum laugh and taking great care of her.

Richard McCann. 44. I will never forget what you did for my Mum that day, coming to visit her and reading your book Just a Man to her. It gave her so much strength. Also for what you have done for me over the years. Thank you for your kind contribution again with my Mum's book.

Demi Turner for being a friend, soul mate and taking care of me when I was at the most vulnerable part of my life and for the laughter, tears, joy, happiness and great memories, especially on the way back from Morocco, sunburned on the plane, chatting bubbles to the lady, lol. May you go forth and multiply your love and light with your Reiki and Lotus Healing. "Proud of you." Always remember that.

Veronica Simister for being a fantastic friend. The affirmations are perfect for the book. Thanks to you, sister.

Vashti Whitefield for her kindness and helping write the foreword. It is a funny old world and I would never have imagined our paths crossing. Still, thanks to your beautiful husband Andy Whitfield and the fantastic Be Here Now documentary on Netflix coming into my life I have an amazing Australian friend and I look forward to sharing a bottle of red